BECOMING
ACTIVIST

CRITICAL PRAXIS AND CURRICULUM GUIDES

Shirley R. Steinberg and Priya Parmar
Series Editors

Vol. 6

The Critical Praxis and Curriculum Guides series
is part of the Peter Lang Education list.
Every volume is peer reviewed and meets
the highest quality standards for content and production.

PETER LANG
New York • Bern • Frankfurt • Berlin
Brussels • Vienna • Oxford • Warsaw

ELIZABETH BISHOP

BECOMING ACTIVIST

CRITICAL LITERACY AND YOUTH ORGANIZING

PETER LANG
New York • Bern • Frankfurt • Berlin
Brussels • Vienna • Oxford • Warsaw

Library of Congress Cataloging-in-Publication Data
Bishop, Elizabeth.
Becoming activist: critical literacy and youth organizing / Elizabeth Bishop.
pages cm. — (Critical praxis and curriculum guides; vol. 6)
Includes bibliographical references.
1. Literacy programs—New York (State)—New York—Case studies.
2. Critical pedagogy—New York (State)—New York—Case studies.
3. Youth—New York (State)—New York—Political activity—Case studies.
4. Social justice—Study and teaching—New York (State)—New York—Case studies.
I. Title.
LC153.N48B57   374'.0124097471—dc23   2014048989
ISBN 978-1-4331-2686-4 (hardcover)
ISBN 978-1-4331-2685-7 (paperback)
ISBN 978-1-4539-1487-8 (e-book)
ISSN 2166-1367 (print)
ISSN 2169-5687 (online)

Bibliographic information published by **Die Deutsche Nationalbibliothek**.
Die Deutsche Nationalbibliothek lists this publication in the "Deutsche Nationalbibliografie"; detailed bibliographic data are available
on the Internet at http://dnb.d-nb.de/.

© 2015 Peter Lang Publishing, Inc., New York
29 Broadway, 18th floor, New York, NY 10006
www.peterlang.com

All rights reserved.
Reprint or reproduction, even partially, in all forms such as microfilm, xerography, microfiche, microcard, and offset strictly prohibited.

TABLE OF CONTENTS

Acknowledgments	vii
Chapter 1. Drop Knowledge Project in New York City	1
Chapter 2. Step One: Mobilizing to Disrupt the Commonplace	13
Chapter 3. Historicizing the Future of Critical Literacy	27
Chapter 4. Step Two: Interrogating Complex Perspectives	39
Chapter 5. Organizing a Space for Justice	53
Chapter 6. Step Three: Identifying Sociopolitical Issues	61
Chapter 7. Designing Ethical Research	73
Chapter 8. Step Four: Taking Social Justice Action	83
Chapter 9. Imagining Tactically Strategic Futures	95
Chapter 10. Step Five: Reflecting and Envisioning Activisms	109
Chapter 11. Articulating Activist Identities	121
References	129

ACKNOWLEDGMENTS

Many inspiring people contributed to the creation, production, and distribution of this book. Thanks are due to everyone at the University of Pittsburgh School of Education, in particular the faculty, staff, and students in the Department of Instruction and Learning. Special thanks are due to a group of extraordinary intellectuals: my longtime advisor Dr. John Myers, currently at Florida State University, who understood my interdisciplinary inclinations and assisted me every step of the way on this research journey; the wonderful Dr. Patricia Crawford at the University of Pittsburgh, who played a crucial role in the completion of this study; Dr. Kim Gomez at the University of California, Los Angeles, who expertly oversaw my apprenticeship into the world of the academy, all the while supporting my radical sensibilities; Dr. Michael Gunzenhauser at the University of Pittsburgh, who reignited the poststructuralist fire in my brain when we first met in 2009; Dr. Matt Luskey at the California Polytechnic State University, who encouraged my concept mapping and advised me through my experiments into and against forms of academic writing; and the estimable Shakespearean and queer theorist, Dr. Madhavi Menon at American University, one of my earliest advisors, whose own deconstructed writing and intellectual free play continues to mesmerize and inspire me. I could not have hoped for a more diverse, energetic, expert, supportive, and brilliant group of advisors guiding me through the dissertation marathon that resulted in this manuscript. The students at the University of Pittsburgh, both my doctoral colleagues and my student teachers, brought much peace and good humor to my learning and teaching. Special thanks go out to my classmates/compatriots: Stephanie Kane-Mainier, Susanna Benko, Maritza Lozano, April Mattix, and Elissa Shoaf.

The rich world of educators and youth I know in and around New York City continues to inspire me daily. Special thanks are due to Molly Delano, Eris Johnson-Smith, Coco Killingsworth, Tene Howard, Kevin Murungi, Eddie Mandhry, Savith Sampath, Nassim Zerriffi, Usman Farooq, Evie Hantzopolous, Carol Artigiani, and everyone at Global Kids, Inc., who taught me to educate for social justice and who dialogued with me about this research in its earliest designs. Numerous other educators and scholars have pushed me in thinking and working with youth; shout-outs are due to the guru Billy Dusenberry, the mayor Regina Anderson, 42R ruckus crew GT & CE, and NYC artists-in-residence the honorable Robyn Hamaguchi, Esq., and Dr. Deb Vischak.

I am humbled to have worked with some remarkably creative and committed young people, starting with my earliest work with the Undecided Bananas and the Arts family in the Bronx (RIP Ivan). I have learned so much, from the 12th-grade cultural critics at Columbia University to the young rockers, techies, and writers I worked with in the Lower East Side. The youth I worked with through Global Kids programs were by far some of the most talented people I have ever met. The participants in the Human Rights Activist Project sparked the idea for this study in the first place. It is for and because of the work of youth activists outside of schools that I do the research that I do. Thank you to all of the youth and community activists who have taught me that, in the words of Thich Nhat Hanh, "what we have to learn from each other is how similar we are."

One group of individuals made it possible for this project to happen at all. Thank you to my collaborators: Green Strawberries, Vaga De Franx, Awesome Woman, Gentle Meadows, and People's Republic of Mars. Your powerful words, work, and action spark futurity. You continue to inspire me, and I hope I have done justice to your power on these pages.

I follow a powerful tradition of academics, intellectuals, and anti-institutionalists who foreground acts of love in peaceful struggle. I recognize that I am standing on the shoulders of giants, many of whom are represented in the citations of this text. I have great adoration for my contemporaries in the fight for educational justice, who make me ever more hopeful about the future. A special thank you to Dr. Yolanda Sealey-Ruiz at Teachers College, who serves as a wonderful friend and mentor to me in my position as a public intellectual. Everyone in the Office of Teacher Education, specifically the Peace Corps Fellows Program, was gracious and supportive as I finished this project. Countless thanks to Nicolas Stahelin, who brought me to Teachers College and to many unexpected opportunities.

Chris Myers and everyone at Peter Lang Publishing made this process simple. Thanks to series editors Dr. Shirley Steinberg and Dr. Priya Parmar for providing this platform for critical praxis. I am humbled to be amongst the critical voices in this series. Also, thanks are due to the editors of the *Journal of Curriculum Theorizing*, who published an earlier version of Chapter 3 on critical literacy, and to the editors of *Theory in Action*, who published an earlier version of Chapter 11 on articulation theory.

Endless thanks go out to my family, who support me in all that I pursue. I take my lead from my educator family: my parents, Richard and Kathleen Bishop, and my sister Jane Bishop Marcoux, who taught me what it means to work hard to forward equitable and exciting learning opportunities for young people; and my brother Peter Bishop, who taught me how to hustle to be successful from as early as I can remember. Thank you for always believing in me.

Finally, my greatest thanks goes to Britney Harsh. Thank you for talking me through endless revision. I never could have written this book without you. *Pura vida.*

· 1 ·

DROP KNOWLEDGE PROJECT IN NEW YORK CITY

Vaga De Franx: On any given event, when people ask me, "What do you really do?" I say, "Well, we organized for about four months. We connected, we flyered our campuses, we talked to people, we tirelessly outreached to professors, we annoyed administration, and annoyed security for months. And we did it with the idea in our minds that there were other students in other campuses who were doing the same and we had an opportunity to secure that community on our campuses because there was somebody on another campus doing the same."

This text tours a 2012 literacy study of urban youth activism in New York City. As the primary investigator and author, I am joined in my narration by the five youth participants: Vaga De Franx, Gentle Meadows, Green Strawberries, Awesome Woman, and People's Republic of Mars (all names are self-selected pseudonyms). These five young activists are alumni of the Human Rights Activist Project (HRAP), a social action-oriented youth organizing program run by Global Kids (GK). They are all in their early twenties and come from historically underresourced NYC neighborhoods and public schools. Their language is central to understanding their experiences in this cultural studies research project, and you will read excerpts of their words at length throughout.

When I first met with each of these youth activists to explain the project and gauge their interest, one recurring idea that echoed across our conversations was the notion of collectivity. Awesome Woman spoke of organizing a student union for all students of color at her university. Vaga De Franx discussed building a citywide student coalition of activists for access to education. Green Strawberries was talking about Occupy Wall Street, People's Republic of Mars about public health, and Gentle Meadows about community literacy projects and socially just investiture. All of these activists engage their local communities, forwarding various approaches to human rights-based popular education built around justice, equity, care, and peaceable coexistence.

Full disclosure: I received an Educator Fellowship from Global Kids as a NYC public high school teacher in the mid-2000s. I went to work for the organization as a Senior Educator the following year, at which time I cofacilitated a branch of HRAP in Brooklyn at the High School for Global Citizenship (HSGC). Although I am no longer employed by the organization, I continue to publicly support their work with young people in NYC and with youth internationally. I am happy to publish this book as GK celebrates 25 years of successful youth development work.

It is important to note that no participants in this research study attended HSGC. I came to know each of the youth activists in this study over time, through HRAP citywide happenings at GK headquarters on the East Side of Manhattan, and at various leadership events located around New York. Thus, the shared background of the five activists in this research was their participation in HRAP when they were in various other high schools across the city. It is their diverse experiences in human rights activism and social justice organizing that made them excellent candidates for participation in this literacy study.

I use the term "youth" in relation to the participants although all were over 18 when they agreed to be involved in the study. Youth is itself a political term, one that recognizes the power of young people not as "kids" to be controlled and "children" to be quieted but as growing adults who possess the capacity to be leaders in the present. Although the study focuses on the past, on their histories and memories as youth activists, their trajectories clearly point to a great future as they become adult human rights leaders.

Research at the Intersection of Literacy and Activism

This study, named the Drop Knowledge Project in New York City (DKPNYC), is an activist pursuit in and of critical literacy research. Critical literacy is both a theory and practice of teaching and learning, involving an intentional study of difference, becoming conscious of one's own experience, considering multiple perspectives on social and political topics, and acting to redress inequity and oppression (Janks, 2013; Lankshear & McLaren, 1993; Morrell, 2007). While critical literacy has been historically theorized within the context of formal education, research shows there are substantial limitations to conducting such overtly political work inside of schools (Beck, 2005; Freesmith, 2006; Luke & Dooley, 2007).

In turn, this study was designed to understand critical literacy in activist spaces where organizing happens outside of school. From a survey of the literature across the two areas of study, there are important connections but limited research on the operations of literacy in the development of youth as social justice activists (see Ardizzone, 2007; Blackburn & Clark, 2007). What is not welldefined are the critically literate skills of such activist work for future organizing and/or the creation of replicable learning models.

Of course, the term "activist" is something of an explosive one. I chose to study the critically literate practices through which urban youth activists discern, dissect, debunk, respect, and create media, artifacts, and social actions in response to operations of injustice that they witness and experience. From local and immediate acts such as campaigning to combat bullying in city schools and police racial profiling in city streets to lobbying against state and federal policies that deny undocumented youth opportunities to access higher education, youth activists are rising up. Such activism has yet to be purposefully investigated in relation to literacy learning. I began my first interview with each participant with one necessary baseline question: "Do you consider yourself an activist?"

Gentle Meadows:	I mean, I do. I like to think of the term as broadly as possible. Activist. Organizing I think is more specific but activist should be an umbrella term. I feel like now, in society, when someone talks about an activist, it's normally painted in a negative light. And I don't think it should be that way. It connects a lot of people in a lot of ways. I don't know how I would define it. Socially aware, that is definitely one term to associate it with. Engaging with the community, with your surroundings. Trying to realize people have different goals, but it is the process that links you with another person together.
Awesome Woman:	I do. Even though I feel like sometimes I'm not an active activist, those activism roots are sort of always

	in me and they are–they come out and people are always surprised by it. There are a lot of things that I don't accept about the way things are, how people talk to each other, and how they interact.
Green Strawberries:	I do consider myself an activist, but I also consider myself more of an organizer than an activist. Because activism means that you are just pretty much aware, you are conscious and you may do some work here and there, but being an organizer is when you go really in-depth into issues. Activism is you show up. Organizer is you make it happen so that other people can show up which is, I think, the main—huge—difference.
Vaga De Franx:	Ah, yes, I do. I do consider myself more of an organizer but I do realize that I am an activist.
People's Republic of Mars:	Absolutely. Activism doesn't have a particular medium. It could be anywhere.

Genealogical Roots of the Drop Knowledge Project

This research was designed as a project in nomadology. The Merriam-Webster dictionary defines nomads as individuals who roam with no fixed residence. Poststructuralist philosophers Deleuze and Guattari (1987) used nomadology to make sense of travels into, out of, and through conceptual landscapes with real implications. In such a schema, conceptual nomads survive like guerrilla gardeners; they prove the value in planting seeds in empty lots and "getting lost" (Lather, 2007) from time to time.

Before I left New York City in 2009 to go back to study in Pittsburgh, I created a codex of concept maps, processing potential directions for learning I hoped to undertake as a cultural theorist in the wide field of "language, literacy, and culture." Upon rereading, it's easy to see how my initial ideas about ethics, politics, and humanizing literacy pedagogies have been transformed and translated here. My development as a researcher necessitated my intellectual wandering, but that early spirit and intention is everpresent in this work. At the time I was writing these ideas, I was finishing my brief tenure working at Global Kids, where GK youth were frequently "dropping knowledge" into the learning space, spitting wisdom and challenging forms of a discriminatory status quo:

Green Strawberries:	What is radical? Really, actually, radical is not even that radical if you really think about it. Equality—that is considered radical. Why, you know? Fuck—class. That is considered radical. But is it really?

This study (and the larger activist research project that has grown out of it) is named after these young people and youth like them everywhere who practice ethical action across spaces of radical difference (Welch, 1991). By working in participatory ways with DKPNYC participants, I sought to provide a forum for research that supported these youth activists to broadcast their positions and their messages, to counternarrate, peer-educate, and connect with others involved in the same, yet always different struggles.

To do so, I focus explicitly on praxis throughout. Praxis is defined here through Freire (1970) as a process of naming the conditions of oppression and struggling collectively with others in a cycle of action-reflection-action against such oppression. Critical literacy theorists Lankshear and McLaren (1993) argued that a guiding principle behind "transformative critical literacy praxis" involves "attempting to understand how agents working within established structures of power participate in the social construction of literacies, revealing their political implications" (p. 7).

To extend activist explorations of literacy further, this book discusses relevant research on both critical literacy and youth organizing. In the remainder of this chapter, I briefly address literacy, activism, and research. I return to these topics explicitly in the alternating chapters that follow. With an intentional focus on the language of the youth activists, I introduce you to the participants in depth in Chapter 2, and you meet them continuously over the course of the entire book. You'd be lucky to meet them in person, to dialogue with them and their peers as they grapple with some of the most crucial issues of our contemporary moment, to experience them dropping knowledge on you. Of course, these are just five out of innumerable youth in the U.S. and internationally who are organizing for the future of a peaceable, habitable planet. It is my hope that reading the words of these young human rights activists will spark futurity and will propel others fearlessly into the beautiful struggle of perpetual justice-based learning and organizing.

Becoming Critically Literate

Critical literacy is a kind of literacy about structures, about structural violence, and understanding operations of power systems. It is built on the exploration of personal, sociopolitical, economic, and intellectual borders. It recognizes the situated nature of experience and creates a pedagogy of (dis) location where learners are positioned to operate as "border crossers" (Giroux, 2005). It is grounded in the imperative to examine the contradictions in society between the meaning of freedom, the demands of social justice, the obligations of citizenship, and the structured silences that permeate incidences of oppression in the everyday. Critical literacy uses texts and production skills in ways that enable students to examine the social and cultural politics of daily life, enabling them to actively seek out contradiction and respond with inclinations toward peace and justice.

It is important to maintain deferral in defining critical literacy. Since the 1980s, critical literacy theorists have outlined emancipatory theories of learning (Freire & Macedo, 1987) that addressed the complex relations of power, language, and oppression through social critique, advocacy, and cultural transformation (Knoblauch & Brannon, 1993). Educational researchers discuss critical literacy as a theory of social practice, as the negotiation and creation of meaning in the interest of social justice (Greene, 2008; Nieto, 1999; Provenzo, Jr., 2005). While there is no single model of critical literacy (as there is no single model of youth organizing), the emphasis on praxis has offered participants a concept through which to construct meanings that support their literacy for civic engagement (Lankshear & McLaren, 1993). Recently, Janks (2010) has echoed the notion of critical literacy as both a shifting skill set and embodied social practice, highlighting the need for learners to engage with multiple cultural values to facilitate more justice-oriented understandings of both self and other.

I approach literacy learning as an activist educator and researcher. There is a long and interesting (anti)tradition of activist researchers (see, for example, Cancian, 1993; Hale, 2006; Naples, 2011). Provenzo, Jr. (2005) called it an activist practice to ask questions that critically interrogate, interpret, and contextualize the ways in which people can be empowered and disempowered. He argued that all learners should ask questions about who speaks in a culture, who defines literacy, and whose knowledge is included in defining and creating curricula in learning communities. Recent scholarship on critical literacy reifies the emphasis on understanding the social and historical factors influencing social (in)justices, answering Freire's (1970) oft-evoked call to "read the world."

Across the last decade of research, five overlapping components have been consistently articulated as "core principles" for cycles of critical literacy (Comber & Simpson, 2001), frequently conceived of as the "transformative elements" in critical literacy pedagogy (Lewison, Flint, & Van Sluys, 2002).

I have synthesized these concepts from across the literature as: (a) mobilizing learners as social actors with knowledge and skills to disrupt the commonplace; (b) conducting research, analysis, and interrogation of multiple viewpoints on an issue; (c) identifying issues focused on sociopolitical realities in the context of the lives of the learners; (d) designing and undertaking actions focused on social justice outside of the classroom; and (e) reflecting upon actions taken and creating vision(s) for future project(s). This taxonomy of critical literacy praxis outlines five tenets that researchers, educators, and youth have used in various ways across the existing literature to define their own projects, in their own contexts, on their own terms.

Youth Activist Organizing

Youth organizing is a relatively new field of research, a hybrid space that is both academic and activist in terms of content foci and methodological approaches. Contemporary youth organizing projects offer a space for both the individual and collective development of civic, activist, and other identities. Youth organizing is a field worthy of greater attention in relation to urban studies in education because it has been identified as one of the only spaces for urban youth to position themselves as agents of sociopolitical power with tools to exercise that power in their interest (Ginwright, 2010b).

The phenomenon of youth organizing emerges from a long history of youth activism in the United States (see Bartoletti 1999; Gordon, 2010; Hoose, 2001). Various youth development practitioners, sociologists, and urban educators have begun to identify the personal, cultural, and social benefits of designing community organizing into youth development programming. Scholars including Ginwright and James (2002), Noguera (2003), Fine (1994), Anyon (2005), and numerous others have identified the need for youth leadership through civic engagement learning experiences that challenge archaic notions of passive civility and institutional verticality. In relation to urban education, these authors have all supported calls for participatory social inquiry and action research with youth that lead to a range of social shifts calibrated toward equity and justice.

When youth engage in campaign development, outreach, and peer education, they exercise practices of critical literacy for local civic action, learning about and navigating their complex surroundings while building relationships with their peers and adult allies. In the process, youth participants develop skills to conduct community research, pursue issue development, and undertake political analysis, direct action, and focused reflection. By speaking at community meetings, lobbying for public policy initiatives, and holding demonstrations, youth engage in advanced forms of leadership opportunities and exercise their problem-solving skills in authentic sociopolitical contexts of speaking and writing. Ginwright (2003) found that when urban youth organizers identify needs in their communities and articulate their collaborative vision for social change, they utilize analytic tools and foster critical perspectives that result in a greater sense of self-efficacy and civic responsibility.

The literature on youth organizing intersects in complex ways with critical literacy. As a context for critical education, youth organizing projects take on forms of critical literacy when youth: (a) identify community issues for thematic investigation; (b) participate in and conduct social movement history research and political education workshops; (c) engage in collective organizing and media trainings; and (d) participate in campaign development, community outreach, strategic action, and intentional reflection. The latest research in relation to youth organizing has demonstrated connections to increased civic engagement (Christens & Dolan, 2011), greater investment in school-based learning (Heinz, 2012), and higher rates of matriculation to postsecondary education (Shah, 2011). Mira (2013) demonstrated that youth organizing is an ideal model for promoting student engagement. Mira's work showed that when learning pedagogies are simultaneously designed around personal development and community awareness, they enable active engagement of youth around social, political, cultural, and economic issues. What remains unknown are the critically literate practices youth engage with as organizers. This research begins to fill that gap.

Asking Research Questions

There are two research questions (and related subquestions) that frame this study and guide the theoretical framework and methodological design described in subsequent chapters:

1. How do urban youth organizers engage in critical literacy praxis as they become activists?

a. What do urban youth organizers *read and research* to identify issues for activism and organizing?
b. In what ways do urban youth organizers *consume, critique, and respond* to texts? How do these literate practices inform their activist work?
c. How do urban youth organizers *create* texts to support their activism? What kinds of texts do they produce; how do they *disseminate* their work; to what audience(s); with what purpose(s)?
2. How do urban youth organizers articulate a vision of themselves as activists?
  a. How do urban youth organizers define activism? How do these definitions relate to their articulation of their identities as activists?
  b. What relationships do urban youth organizers have to the texts and contexts of activism and organizing?

These questions are answered through the taxonomy of critical literacy, using qualitative interview data from conversations with the youths themselves. The answer to how we "become activists" will, in the end, remain elusive. This is intentional. I did not write this study to attempt an absolute codification or classification of the *how* and *why* of activism. Creating such a research write-up would, to a certain extent, violently etch a method or impose a model for replication onto youth organizing. I have no such intent toward totalization. Such claims to generalizable representations would undermine the very specific, personal, and fluid experiences of local activists, such as the alumni of the Human Rights Activist Project (HRAP) documented in this text. I purposefully resist these moves as ones that rigidize the nomadic and divergent acts of activist collaboration.

The only answer I will affirm is that the "essence" of what it means to be an activist is importantly unidentifiable. If this was not the case, activism would be nothing more than its own negation, functioning within replicable representative confines of institutionalized knowledge that control from the clinical to the diagnostic. Attempting to encapsulate what it means to "act" as "activist" is both redundant and absurd. In many ways, the identifier of "activist" is but a moniker, an identity that is alternately vilified, romanticized, and reproached in mainstream American media and across the world.

Instead, I wrote this book to report upon the multiplicity of activist identities, refracted through the notion of the ethical in literacy research design. Whereas more prescriptive approaches might reify false essentialisms about the participants through the interpretation and categorization of their actions and motivations, this study was designed to respect the dignity and subjectivity of participants as experts of their own experience and makers of their own meaning. This research is significant because of its layered schema, documenting urban youth activists as they learn about issues of injustice and intentionally build communities around justice, care, and healing.

Poststructuralist Articulation

Chantal Mouffe's (1993) articulation theory is a framework useful for understanding the constitution of sociopolitical identities—such as that of activist. Through her poststructuralist ontology of political theory, Mouffe forwarded a conception of radical democratic citizenship that is focused on the embodied actions of individual subjects in pluralistic democratic politics. It is here that she introduced articulation theory to account for how individual subjective identities emerge from social discourses. Mouffe's use of articulation theory supports the development of an ontology of democratic citizenship through an analysis of reflexive agency, a will to act, and an ethical ability to make room for the adversary in one's actions. For Mouffe, the effect of articulation is that the subject invokes her or his identity, drawing upon discursive forms that are always only partial. It is in the inability to fully determine the identities of subjects and practices in terms of a fixed discourse that allows for the engendering of dynamic sociopolitical spaces with greater choice and agency.

Mouffe's equation of articulation theory essentially states that relational elements (signifiers that lack meaning in themselves) achieve significance (social meaning) when articulated by and through social discourse in moments of sociohistorical contexts. For each of the participants in this study, their different understandings of activism and themselves as activists were created through moments in their lives. Extracting elements such as tactics, organizations, interlocutors, issues, texts, and locations is key to understanding how participants define themselves as activists in relation to their moment. From running teach-ins and staging boycotts to organizing protests and lobbying politicians, these young people created meaning in relation to their moment.

The central point as applied to this specific research relates to the articulation of identities in fluid discursive spaces of human rights activism. Moments of activism exist in multiple instantiations, where signification is best understood as continually shifting. Mouffe's work is useful in this study by complicating struggles over meaning and value around terms such as "social justice" and processes such as civil disobedience. Looking through these few moments, it is possible to decipher elements of youth becoming activist. Mouffe's work has been written about in relationship to critical pedagogy, to teach youth to adapt to changing discourse positions while enhancing reflexive agency, empowerment, and social responsibility (Nadesan & Elenes, 2008).

To understand this articulation, I applied Mouffe's articulation theory as one hybrid element of analysis that accounts for individual subjective identities emerging from and through discursively created social spaces. Analysis through articulation theory involves a process of identifying social meaning (such as activist identities), where meaning is discursively constituted through the practice of linking relational "elements" (differences) to one another to define them against each other. These elements, which lack meaning in themselves, become meaningful only when articulated by and through a social discourse that enacts transformation into "moments" (of activism). Mouffe delineated element from moment to make the point that a particular signifier only achieves significance in specific sociohistorical contexts of discursive articulation. I use the framework of articulation as a nontotalizing summation, extending my analysis beyond an acute literacy focus. In doing so, I identified connections and divergences between participants' articulation of their activist identities, the contexts where they organize, and the material conditions through which they form their subjectivities.

Scope of the Book

The text is intentionally polyvocal, and the voices of the five young people feature prominently. As literacy research, this study adds to understanding about learning in organizing spaces. By analyzing the discourse of the five participants in the chapters that follow, I identify ways in which youth engage in critical literacy praxis as they build their subjectivity within activist communities. By focusing on literacy outside of school, this work contributes to research on community-based contexts that possess the capacity to educate young people intersubjectively. In the process, they learn about sociopolitical issues and begin to articulate their identities and positionality through social justice-oriented actions.

The structure of the book is rhizomatic, offering multiple entry points through a double articulation around literacy and organizing. The chapters alternate between deep dives into the transcribed interview data with the five youth activists and research writing around existing literature on these interconnected topics. The alternating chapters introduce the youth in their own words, celebrating their subjectivity while exploring their critical literacy learning in their approaches to organizing. Used alternately throughout the text, these chapters serve as interludes to develop in the reader an appreciation for how these five urban youth organizers make sense of their identities as human rights activists. This provides a rich, layered account of the organizers in context, acknowledging the complex ethics, aesthetics, and politics of each individual.

The book is divided into eleven chapters. This first chapter can be imagined as a (de)centered vector from which the text returns and diverges. Chapters 2, 4, 6, 8, and 10 introduce the participants through the five elements of the critical literacy taxonomy. Chapters 3 and 5 look at critical literacy and youth organizing, respectively, tracing the past, present, and future of such political educational work. Chapter 7 presents a discussion of ethical-political approaches to creating and conducting educational research. Chapter 9 offers implications from this study for future research designs and pedagogical initiatives. Chapter 11 (re)presents a meditation on articulation, revisiting the five youth activists who make up the Drop Knowledge Project in New York City. The book is full of rich examples organized around and articulated through individual activisms of each youth.

As an author in a Critical Praxis series, I take seriously the mandate to create a workbook that is accessible for practitioners, a tactical manual for community-based learning, literacy-centered resistance work and activist self-writing. My intention in writing is to offer insight into this rich learning space to support a sustainable future for social justice-oriented youth organizers and educators. To do so, this book aims to teach and learn lessons on disruptive power, to introduce joy as a vital metaphor for continued convergence, and to posit a postfoundational queer theory for future ethical activism.

· 2 ·

STEP ONE: MOBILIZING TO DISRUPT THE COMMONPLACE

Mapping Rhizomatic Research Lines

In this chapter, I begin to map out the trajectories of the five individual youth organizers becoming activist. The present participle form of the word "becoming" is important here because it points to the continual shifting and deferral in defining one's self. Likewise, "activist" is both singular and plural in acknowledging the individual and multiple iterations of activisms. I aim to explore both the distinctiveness of their lives and the plurality that emerges from their foci on collectivity and shared struggle. I start with Vaga De Franx and take a nonnarrative tour through our discursive exchanges, using interview dialogue data to guide our understandings. I repeat this cycle with Gentle Meadows, Green Strawberries, People's Republic of Mars, and Awesome Woman. As self-reportage was key in keeping with the ethical-political schema of this study, participants are quoted at length to support the notion, well matched for research built around transgressive validity (Lather, 2007), that there is value in letting the data speak for themselves (Gould, 1981).

    I focus particularly on the critical literacy praxis through which they engage in the work of activism and organizing. Data collected from each participant were organized first through the taxonomy of critical literacy. The five categories of this taxonomy are provided with varying subsection titles to reflect the differing themes that emerged in dialogue with each participant. The data from the interviews were coded through this taxonomy and excerpts that were selected for publication best fit the realm of these categories, offering polyvocal organizing insights.

The first element in the critical literacy lens I applied is "the ability to mobilize the learner as a social actor with knowledge and skills to disrupt the commonplace." An implicit precursor to this study of activism was that all of the participants self-identified as activists. As such, I did not look specifically at how others mobilized them, but rather I look explicitly at how and why they mobilized themselves. While it is beyond the scope of this chapter to unpack the dynamics and assumptions around the learner, the social, the commonplace, and what qualifies as disruptive (Pivens, 2011), such queries are nonetheless important. The contested discourses around these terms must be named and explored in order to look at the divergent intentions and motivations driving the actions of these youths as they find their activist selves organizing for positive social change.

Vaga De Franx: Mobilizing to Disrupt the Commonplace

Before I began this research, I spoke to some Global Kids staff and snowball sampled suggestions as to which youth activists might be interested in participating in the study. In nearly all of my conversations, Vaga De Franx came up. Although she and I didn't know each other particularly well, I was fortunate that she was so eager, insightful, and willing to participate. I came to learn it was emblematic of her spirit as an organizer and an activist. Her passion, commitment, and deep sense of justice and care came out during the course of our work together in ways that my writing could never begin to encapsulate.

Vaga De Franx is an undocumented student and community organizer. In each of our meetings, she accentuated the importance of local organizing and the need to understand relevant space for activism in our immediate lives. She was attending a university in the city during the time of the study. Tuition increases had complicated her enrollment plans for the following school year, and she was actively protesting the hikes.

In her day-to-day, Vaga De Franx seeks out information about current social justice struggles, questioning moments and operations of oppression that cut across issues. During our first interview in early spring of 2012, she talked to me about her approach to understanding history and current events:

> VDF: Your question before was where do you get your information from, and I think books. Because even in the university, a lot of my fellow student organizers, you know—the class structure is there and you have to go to class. But in terms of really learning, I don't think any of us look at a textbook and think, "This is what I'm learning." It's more like, independent books and who is publishing these? What press is publishing these? Which is something that I never worried about until now. I need to see who is feeding me this information. So when you see that it is this publishing company who has also published Howard Zinn, then I know I can rely on this information and I'm pretty sure that I want to read this perspective. A lot of things happen to be around Marx, and analyzing Marx, and you know, you don't have to read *Kapital* to think Marx is right [laughing]. That is another thing, in our generation, people reading Marx and you know, they say, "I'm not a communist, not a socialist." But there are smaller books and they give you a better perspective. You know, feminist issues. The *Communion* is a great book on patriarchy and the way that relationships work.

Her nuanced discussion of independent books and publishers raised questions about the purveyors of media, illustrating the knowledge and skills she has developed to seek out perspectives that will add complexity to her learning around political economy and history. She asked questions about textual intentions and the intersectional positions of writers, readers, and distributors. Implicit in her referencing of Howard Zinn is the acknowledgment of his work as a progressive scholar and a "people's historian" whose legacy is connected to publishing alternate ways of seeing, telling, and constructing history. She went on to talk about seeking out multiple perspectives in the media and using mainstream media against itself:

> VDF: *Democracy Now!* I think is a big one and a lot of activists know about it. It is it's own independent news media. And I think that what a lot of activists do is – well, have very little faith in mainstream media. We use media. Like, if we are on the Internet, we see an article and we almost use it to prove our point of what the media wants us to think, what the media wants us to believe, and why they want us to believe that.

Vaga De Franx uses mainstream media in ways that force a meta-critique of underlying messages. She engaged in such critique when discussing her thoughts about the *New York Times*. She recognized that despite the level of professionalism and expertise in the paper, there were biases with what they report, how they report, what they leave out and how one is expected to perceive their articles. She used the example of mainstream media's reporting on illegal weapons trade in Mexico and how it shaped messages to U.S. citizens about Mexicans as the sole, violent perpetrators of the "War on Drugs." Here, she offered alternative ways of understanding the material conditions surrounding U.S.-Mexico relations, a topic that was very personal to her as an activist.

She took this discussion into the issues she organizes around the most: educational equality, immigrant rights, Stop and Frisk, and other forms of "racist police brutality." She also went into an extended aside about environmentalism and the internal struggles of meta-cognitive activisms and activists in making small moves toward sustainability. I asked her how she thought people should learn the history they don't know or don't understand to inform social justice actions:

> VDF: Peer education. Study groups. Being able to, sometimes when I read a book, I get influenced by the writer and I — sometimes even asking the most critical questions, you sometimes can't analyze a book objectively and compare it to other people's ideas or just reality, you know. So, being able to read within a study group and talk about it, it helps so much. It doesn't allow you to just get caught up in that writer's work. It really, like—talking about feminist theory with men has been the most informative thing I have ever been through. Because, as a woman, I am reading the book and I'm just like yes, yes, yes, that's exactly what I go through. And the feminist writer will give me an analysis of why men suck. And why this and why that. And then it's just like, men suck, men suck. And then I talk to a man who is my friend and I'm like, well—you don't suck. [laughs] But you have these ideals too. So, being able to talk about that. That's the best way. That's really the only way, to me.

This emphasis on complex dialogue is a topic that emerged time and again in my many conversations with the participants. Vaga De Franx highlights the value of sharing perspectives to make sense of ideas, to include disparate voices to help oneself to gain a more just, measured perspective across issues of gender, ethnicity, and social class.

Gentle Meadows: Quietly Disrupting the Peace

Gentle Meadows is a soft-spoken, young queer man. He recently graduated from a liberal arts college in the Hudson Valley of New York, completing his

STEP ONE: MOBILIZING TO DISRUPT THE COMMONPLACE   17

degree in three years. He majored in political science with a minor in international studies. He is distinguished by his humility, and he was initially shy to discuss himself and his accomplishments in any great detail. He began by talking in brief about his life history:

> GM: I'm from New York City; I grew up in New York City. I went to an inner-city public high school. I grew up in a lot of neighborhoods. I moved around a lot in New York City neighborhoods where it was primarily immigrants living in them. Elmhurst in Queens, and Sunnyside—that's where I went to middle school, in Queens again. Jackson Heights, in Queens again. And now in the Upper East Side with my mom. I mean, that last one is not primarily immigrant populated, but the others are.

He was excited to participate in the DKPNYC study because he has known me and my former coworker from Global Kids for quite a while: "I feel like you guys have been part of who I am today as an activist and a person who thinks with these ideas." This personal connection was clear as he spoke in greater detail about the formal and informal conversations we had while he was in GK.

> GM: Yeah, it's a good thing. I mean, with your work at Global Kids and even the programs–I mean I feel like that is a very foundational part of why I think of things this way today. It's not just the programs themselves, but also the conversations and how it expands to other than that specific time and place.

Gentle Meadows said that he didn't know what he would add to the project at first because he didn't consider himself well versed on anything "critical." As he said that, he went into a lengthy aside about critical security studies and the focus of his research for his undergraduate thesis comparing human security to national security. "So, um, I got a little bit [of knowledge] there but I wouldn't say I am a pro at Marx or anything," he said, laughing the thought away.

When he graduated from high school, Gentle Meadows attended "a super liberal arts school" upstate. He critiqued his university heavily throughout the course of our conversation. Although he is quiet upon first introductions, Gentle Meadows is deeply inquisitive, questioning the status quo and asking tough questions about the current state of domestic and foreign policy. As an activist, he organizes around issues related to "access to education," a phrase he used many times throughout our dialogues:

GM: I wish that [teachers] would ask more open-ended questions, especially in the humanities and in literature. Because those never have—I mean yes there is recorded history, but history has always been written, primarily, by the winners. And you need to always question that. I mean, maybe this isn't, or wasn't, the major perspective on this particular issue in a certain period of time. But, I don't know—seeing other point of views is important.

I met Gentle Meadows when he was a senior in a high school in Queens. During the school year that followed, we explored many complex topics together, examining multiple perspectives on current events with a deep historical context. So much of GK's pedagogy is designed around interpersonal, interactive, and informal learning. Through our dialogues and workshops, we considered multiple perspectives on current events and created space for (re) considering one's own position(s):

GM: Yeah, from food production to the wars in Afghanistan and Iraq, the Israeli-Palestinian issue which was a very hot topic, and women's rights. Um, I remember we did an LGBTQI day, which was also very controversial for the people there.
EB: Why was it controversial? I mean I remember, but for you.
GM: Like, so in the two high schools combined, I would say the majority of students come from immigrant backgrounds. So I would say on issues of immigration and things like that they would be more progressive. But on other issues, like cultural issues, they would be like—whether women should be treated equally as men. And acceptance of, not just tolerance, but acceptance of lesbians, gays, bisexuals, transgendered, intersex people. It's more up in the air. Some people do and some people don't care. Some people don't know. So that dialogue definitely helps there. Books wouldn't change that if you are just reading them alone. They need to be discussed and—you just need to talk with other people.

Here we went back in our shared memory to a time when we explored underlying messages of bigotry and oppression through the use of inquiry-based language that questioned the textual intentionality behind prejudiced thought and action. The workshop he referenced was about homophobia and heterosexism and asked participants to read dialogues that turned moral verbiage of heteronormativity around on the straight world.

I remember Gentle Meadows as quite daring that day, uncharacteristically extroverted as he argued for equality for sexual minorities. It was a memorable example of disrupting the commonplace at his school in Queens. So much of what could be qualified as disruptive about Gentle Meadows is his call for understanding and caring for all people. This was one moment that highlighted his growth as a social activist, an example of him mobilized to challenge the discriminatory status quo and countering the many mainstream messages of judgmental dehumanization.

Green Strawberries: In/Against a Digital Occupation

I don't remember exactly when I first met Green Strawberries. There was a moment when I worked GK citywide events on the weekends where she and Vaga De Franx were very visible. They were friends with Gentle Meadows, who introduced me to her as a young activist interested in feminism, queerness, education, and immigration. Green Strawberries is an undergraduate woman, living in Queens at the time of this research and studying political science at a private college in the city. She has a tendency to question the everyday in a way that operates around and within many borderlands that are at turns moralizing and conscientizing (Freire, 1970). The arc of our dialogue followed her thinking between positions of justice, morality, creation, critique, and right.

We met a few times before I invited her to work on this project. I first visited her at the Bowery Poetry Club, where she was selling her art. When the study began, we met briefly in Union Square to talk about a host of issues: access to higher education, women's studies, assessment in K-12 contexts, public schooling in NYC, and our experiences in the nonprofit world. At the time of our most in-depth interview, she was deeply involved with Occupy Wall Street. We met for a lengthy conversation at a café on the corner of Tompkins Square Park in the East Village. As we talked about Occupy, she was quick to interrogate the benefits of Internet organizing. I troubled the idea of disembodied Internet activism and asked her if she thought online organizing is lacking:

> GS: It definitely loses a lot I think. You can't create a revolution with—the Internet is just a start-up. It should not be where you are going full time. First off, anyone can put anything on the Internet... So you need to know people who are already connected to that [issue] and be like, yo, is this really what is going on? So it really comes back down to knowing someone, right? I definitely feel like it's more important to have, if not a one-on-one, a collective. Post that there is going to be a meeting, this time, this place. Don't start a meeting online, that makes no sense to me. I don't know how

one can get much done that way. It's also, I also feel like it takes away humanity. It's very dehumanizing. And if we are going to try to get to a place of true equality, we are going to need to get to a more human place, right? Which is one thing that I feel like is—I wish people recognized more and that they realized what the Internet is really doing to us and how maybe we shouldn't be so dependent on it for everything. And the other thing is, you put anything on the Internet and the cops will fucking find out, right? You tell another person, in code, the cops are probably not going to find out. That's the other thing I feel like people are probably not getting.

There is a sense of personal indignation in Green Strawberries as she argues against dehumanization. Although she doesn't go into detail about the limits of organizing online, she questions its practice even as she acknowledges the Internet as a revolutionary space for communication and a platform for information freedom. I asked if she had seen pockets of success in her recent organizing experiences, in Zuccotti Park or otherwise:

GS: From my perspective, everything is happening on the Internet. Mostly. A lot of it is happening on the Internet. And then I feel like—because Occupy Wall Street is very interesting. I think it is definitely different from other forms of movements. Because of that, it's not this one unified movement, right? It's literally, like, here's Occupy Wall Street, here's one branch, there's another, sometimes they intertwine but not really...I think that it's not such a good thing. But I feel like that is just how it is going to be for a while. If Occupy Wall Street does go further...Well, the issue with the stemming of branches and what not is the fact that there are all these different views how to go about creating a revolution. Anyone you talk to in Occupy Wall Street, they're always talking about "when we get to the revolution" this is what is going to happen. But the problem is that we all want to get to a revolution in a different way, and so we are all kind of being like, you know you don't really agree with me, I'm going to go over here. Is Occupy Wall Street ever going to go anywhere with that mindset?

Green Strawberries offered some pointed critiques here, locating herself amidst various collectives with multiple views on revolution. She was particularly astute at addressing the fractured factioning that occurs and the detriments of the divisive U.S. political Left caught up in a hyperintellectual paralysis. It was interesting talking to her about the importance of multiple perspectives and the danger of information overload. The shared discourse space of the Internet created a platform for us to use our language to discuss the messages behind the media we consumed online, including online organizing campaigns and the lack of human face-to-face interaction. Throughout our conversation, Green Strawberries explored subtle messages in blunt ways. She simultaneously criticized the white Occupiers for their "G20 chic," questioned the virtues of Internet organizing, and applauded the internationality so immediately accessible through online media.

People's Republic of Mars: Standing for Human Rights

People's Republic of Mars is a young man from Queens. He was finishing his final year at a private university in the city during this research project, having spent the previous year studying abroad in Europe. I asked him if he had any preferred words to identify himself and he answered, "I prefer the word catalyst." He is highly ambitious and has achieved much in his young career as a community organizer and activist. Notably, he founded a nonprofit organization, which he discussed at different times across the study. We talked in great depth about the specificity of organizing online, and he highlighted the larger notion of seeking out multiple perspectives as a form of information activism.

Much of our conversation around social and political organizing deviated toward a discussion of foreign affairs and ways to attain peace through the operations of major international and nongovernmental organizations. A diplomat with the heart of a social justice activist, People's Republic of Mars seeks to disrupt human rights violations in every form. He takes seriously the objectives of the Millennium Development Goals, critiquing various levels of public policy while brainstorming ways to positively impact material conditions for those without access to clean water, healthy food, affordable healthcare, and quality education.

As we began to discuss his history around human rights activism, he questioned the underlying messages of some seminal texts upon which human rights policy is based, particularly looking at the Convention on the Rights of the Child (CRC) and other such frameworks of human rights. He interrogated the concept of hypocrisy and illuminated policy gaps as he talked about the textual intentions driving U.S. human rights agendas:

PRM: And there are things that we do in the U.S. and, you know, Guantanamo, waterboarding, everything. But when other countries do it, we say that it is a violation of human rights. Like, this is also a violation of human rights.

So, we have to be a role model, kind of. If we expect them to do something, we have to do it first and then tell them, all right, we are implementing and you should do it. Like, we haven't signed—what is it called? The—it's the children's human rights.

EB: Oh, the CRC?

PRM: CRC. Right. We haven't signed that yet…Yeah. [extended silence] So we cannot just tell people not to recruit child soldiers. Like, I personally think that child soldiers are, you know, child soldiers are a terrible idea. You know? They force kids to fight. But, as much as I hate those people who recruit child soldiers, I see the other side also. I see that we have not signed, so we cannot just go and tell them "Stop that." You know? We have to do that first, you know…But, I just feel like before we tell them, we have to implement human rights here first.

Awesome Woman: Questioning the Status Quo

In her words: "Awesome Woman is a college student who is incredibly curious about the world. She's particularly interested in community organizing, event planning, race politics, women's rights, literacy, feminism, theater, LGBT identities and issues, postcolonial manifestations of culture and fashion. She spends most of her time organizing several events on campus and loving people. She's plain and simple AWESOME!"

I met Awesome Woman when she was a sophomore in high school. She always struck me as an insightful, outspoken young woman. As you will learn in the pages that follow, Awesome Woman thinks deeply about issues and intelligently challenges social and cultural norms that allow ignorance and hate to go unchallenged and unaddressed.

Across more than six hours of interviews around downtown Manhattan and Brooklyn, I was struck by Awesome Woman's ability to mobilize. She spoke knowledgeably on so many issues, crossing borders between race, gender, religion, sexuality, and citizenship. Through her stories of the past, Awesome Woman described vivid remembrances, current struggles, and future visions. During the course of the study, she directed a number of cultural programs and activist projects at her university, attended a citywide Feminist Bootcamp, and traveled to South Africa on an educational study trip. She talked chronologically about each of these life experiences across our meetings, but I introduce them here discontinuously to highlight emerging themes in her ongoing conversations around prejudice, identity, internationality, and the need for

STEP ONE: MOBILIZING TO DISRUPT THE COMMONPLACE 23

critical education. I asked her if she sees herself disrupting the commonplace frequently, and she laughed that she does. When I asked her how she is disruptive, she focused on her use of language and media to interrogate everyday experience. She told me about her use of video blogs to respond to misogynist messages in local communities, popular culture, and social media:

> AW: So, I did three different ones. One, it was about men and, like, I was on Facebook one day and it was like, "Oh summer's coming. I don't want to see any girls with any folds" and blah blah blah. And I'm just like, shut the fuck up. Who are you to judge? It's not your body, first of all. And if you don't like it, look away. So I made a video about that. And then, I made one about questions. Like me as a woman-identified queer person, how can I judge some male who is, I don't know, who is walking around wearing flip-flops or whatever. And I'm like, "Why are you wearing those? Ew. You shouldn't be wearing them." [laughs] But, why do I need to do that? Why is that any of my business? Why do I need to comment?
>
> EB: It is totally a form of violence, though, right?
>
> AW: It is. It's just wrong. It just promotes—we already have a society that hates bodies and movement and all that stuff.

Awesome Woman questions the operations of status quo moralism. She looks at different points of view and considers multiple perspectives on issues of identity, community, mainstream media, and actively challenges hateful positiontaking. There were many multiple ways in which she was disruptive, interrupting violent discourses and engaging in deep reflection on the actions she has taken and has yet to take. We talked across concepts of language, voice, silence, power, and marginalization in our discussion of her activism and organizing. In early reflection upon the differences between cultures, she extended a critique of human rights:

> AW: It's so interesting when we talk about other peoples, and other countries, and say what they are doing is wrong. How do you know that? You don't live in that society. You know? You don't know what goes into it. I remember I was reading a chapter from this book—my friend is reading this book called "Half the Sky" and I read a chapter and it is about this woman, about a whole bunch of different women and their struggles. And it was about this one woman, who got raped and she ended up being sort of like a Mother Teresa—she has taken women who are battered and she had her own shelter inside her house. So it's like this amazing story about how she overcame and has done all this stuff for other women. And then it says, that she got married and became somebody's second wife. Like, it's not a

problem that she is somebody's second wife but that they put it under as like a joke, you know. Like, she did all of this and then she decided she was going to be a second wife. How sad, how demoralizing, how degrading. You know? And I felt like that was really there, and I was so unnerved about it. Like, why? There is so much we don't understand and we just, our views of human rights are what we consider rights. And we don't take in all of the social and political aspects of things that happen in other places. And it's really horrible. I guess—what am I trying to say? I'm not going to call it Eurocentric, because we're not Europeans, but like—how we believe things should be the same everywhere. But that's not true. And half of the difficulties of having treaties is that. I mean, not that we shouldn't try or shouldn't aim for that. But treaties that like, where all of those countries are supposed to agree upon, like the Geneva Convention.

EB: The CRC.

AW: Exactly. So like, different politics and history. A lot of rich history.

She questions textual intentions around the creation of our identities and our values in relation to these moralistic positions and approaches to thinking about rights. Much of what Awesome Woman said echoed sentiments expressed by People's Republic of Mars, that there needs to be a sense of self-responsibility in a nation's dictates beyond its borders. We took the notion of borders further in discussing history and current events:

AW: There are borders, actual barriers that were put up, that don't make sense.

EB: Like colonized lines?

AW: Yeah, like families who have been separated for centuries because of lines that are superficial or artificial. I'm not sure which word I'm looking for.

EB: Both, I think.

AW: Maybe [laughs]. And then within places, people separate themselves all the time. Within the nation, or whatever. And so now, I'm so interested in South Africa. And there was this really shitty special that I watched the other day. And I was just like, oh, it's on, so let me watch it. And it was called "Global White Woman." And basically, it was an exploration of beauty for white women in South Africa. So I was really so upset. It was basically like this Indian dude who was a self-identified Indian dude, who was basically talking about his obsession with white women and why. And he was so misogynistic, I couldn't even appreciate it. And at the end, I was like why did I watch this? It didn't explore anything that was new to me and I feel like it wasn't new to a lot of audiences. Like, we know white women are beautiful, are considered beautiful in South Africa. But why, really? And who came up with these ideas of beauty? That was not explored.

Awesome Woman speaks with incredible power and insight. She organizes around numerous interconnected issues and speaks at length about their interconnections. She consistently told stories in answer to my questions, responding with deep complexity and an embrace of contradiction as a result of her stance toward continued critical inquiry.

· 3 ·
HISTORICIZING THE FUTURE OF CRITICAL LITERACY

Defining Critical Literacy to Become Critically Literate

Much of the earliest scholarship on critical literacy is based upon Freirean pedagogy. Paulo Freire is the preeminent scholar of critical pedagogy. Freire's text *Pedagogy of the Oppressed* (1970) has proven instructive in focusing on political dimensions of experience and initiating social change with "oppressed" persons by identifying structures of oppression in communities and acting to redress those conditions (see Burbles & Berk, 1999, for discussion). In 1987, Freire and Macedo published their expansive volume on literacy and critical pedagogy. In it, they argued that those who are critically literate can not only understand how meaning is socially constructed within texts but can also come to understand the political and economic contexts in which those texts were created and embedded (Freire & Macedo, 1987).

While Freire and Macedo were perhaps the first to forward an explicit dialogue around the idea of critical literacy, it was not until 1993 that Lankshear and McLaren issued what was to become the seminal text devoted to the topic. In it, they stated that literacy is more complex than the traditionally defined skills of reading and writing. Rather, they argued that such a traditional definition of literacy is ideologically aligned with particular postures of normative sociopolitical consciousness that are inherently oppressive and exploitative. By contrast, critical literacy emphasized the social construction of reading, writing, and text production within political contexts of inequitable economic, cultural, political, and institutional structures. Lankshear and McLaren argued for critically reflective teaching and research agendas in the tradition of Street (1984), focused on both the forms that literate skills take as social practices and the uses to which those skills are employed.

Lankshear and McLaren made a strong distinction between critical literacy and Hirsch's (1988) "cultural literacy," the latter of which dictated a particular corpus of knowledge young people were expected to know to be appropriately informed Americans. Critical literacy seriously challenged this notion of propriety and warned against such a "colonization of culture" (Lankshear & McLaren, 1993, p. 17). The authors argued that critical literacy is an approach to teaching and learning committed to exploring how and why particular social and cultural groups of persons occupy unequal political positions of access to social structures. Rather than promoting any particular reading of any particular group, critical literacy seeks to interrogate the historical and contemporaneous privileging of and exclusion of groups of people and ideas from mainstream narratives. Across their work, there is a lingering concern for doing critical literacy without falling into "colonizing logic" or other forms of theoretical imperialism.

The authors did identify three forms of educational practice that critical literacy can take on, varying by levels of commitment to inquiry and action: liberal education, pluralism, and transformative praxis. Liberal education here means an approach to disciplinary knowledge where intellectual freedom exists and where disparate interpretations are considered, but inevitably contradiction is avoided and rational argumentation within normative structures wins out. In pluralism, there is an emphasis on reading to evaluate principles that support a loose conception of tolerance. Tolerance here is aligned with a notion of diversity that is grounded on benevolence toward those who are not mainstream—and in the process maintains the mainstream. Against these approaches, the authors forwarded "transformative praxis" as that which takes the radical potential of critical literacy into direct emancipatory action in the world.

Tracing the Study of Critical Literacy Theory

In the early 1990s, McLaren and Lankshear were some of the more radical scholars writing on the topic of critical literacy. Around the same time, Apple

(1992) published an essay on "the text and cultural politics" which examined the social legitimation of certain knowledge in schools. Making the argument that "no curriculum is neutral" and that the selection and organization of curricular information is necessarily an ideological process, Apple argued that schools, teachers, and students must study the constructed nature of knowledge about institutions and experiences (whose history and knowledge is replicated by curricular texts and operational contexts) in order to reflectively determine if the school functions as a democratic institution and/or as a site of social control.

Illuminating this struggle in their collection on critical teaching and literacy, Knoblauch and Brannon (1993) outlined four approaches to critical teaching and the idea of literacy learning: functional literacy and the rhetoric of objectivism; interpretive literacy and the politics of nostalgia; expressivism as a literacy for personal growth; and critical literacy. Of these four central approaches, the authors argued that only critical literacy offered the complexity of a sociopolitical framework that foregrounded the study of "the relationships of language and power with practical knowledge of how to use language for advocacy, social critique, and cultural transformation" (Knoblauch & Brannon, 1993, p. 152). This made critical literacy distinct amongst a variety of approaches to literacy learning that claimed to address the sociocultural while remaining intentionally distant from the political.

Across their collection, Knoblauch and Brannon echoed Street's (1984) concern that the tyranny of academic literacies can serve to socially reproduce dominant ideologies (e.g., racism, sexism, classism, homophobia, xenophobia) that perpetuate forms of injustice. Writing that same year, scholars ranging from Hull (1993) to Comber (1993) were beginning to study the implications for critical literacy learning in schools. Comber (2001) later argued that one of the best ways to approach critical literacy is to begin with multiple sources and opposing views to interrogate their construction by specific individuals with particular (always political) goals.

At the turn of the millennium, just before the 2001 reauthorization of the Elementary and Secondary Education Act (ESEA) as the controversial No Child Left Behind Act, Janks (2000) posited four possible orientations for future approaches to critical literacy education based on different perspectives on the relationship between language and power: (a) to understand how language maintains social and political forms of domination; (b) to provide access to dominant forms of language without compromising the integrity of nondominant forms; (c) to promote a diversity which requires attention to the way that uses of language create social identities; and (d) to bring a design perspective that emphasizes the need to use and select from a wide range of available cultural sign systems. Although frequently taken in isolation, Janks argued that it is through the interdependence of these approaches that learners can most fully engage theories and pedagogies of critical literacy.

Contemporary Practices of Critical Literacy

The major emphasis across various critical literacy projects has been a naming of and a willingness to reflect upon the role that language and texts play in the construction of the self and the social. In practice, researchers and educators have articulated and studied critical literacy in a host of different ways. Petrone and Gibney (2005) drew on the work of critical literacy theorists to articulate a "democratic pedagogy" in American literature classrooms, where students investigate and transform their worlds through an inquiry-based examination of culture and society—to consider what is present, what is missing, and what is possible. For Petrone and Gibney, this approach to teaching literature and intertextuality is about "foregrounding historical, cultural, and social issues" in the interest of supporting the development of critical citizens who seek to expand the possibilities of democratic public life (p. 36). They argued that the English language arts curriculum should provide a space for students to deepen their traditional literacy skills while becoming critically skilled "consumers, producers, and distributors of texts and information" (p. 39).

Singer's (2006) text on "writing and reading to change the world" offered a series of stories of justice told through collaborative writing practices. Singer studied students writing about stories of injustice, finding an audience and collaborators while writing themselves into activism. In Singer's study, the youth studied models of expository essays about activists while reading Philip Hoose's (2001) text about the influence of youth throughout the history of the social justice movement in the United States. Writing "toward change," the students were asked: "what does your activist story teach about movement toward making positive social change?" (Singer, 2006, p. 97). As students designed and executed culminating projects on issues of activism, participants became "consumed with the world outside of the school," becoming experts in activism as well as experts in research literacy (Singer, 2006, p. 112).

That same year, Borsheim and Petrone (2006) published a study about "teaching the research paper for local action" in which they framed classroom-based learning through a consideration of how students engage in critical literacies through the consumption, production, and distribution of texts. As classroom teachers, the authors introduced a research paper unit that focused on social action locally, providing students with an opportunity to critically investigate their contexts and respond through the production of texts that promote positive social change. Echoing Freire and Macedo (1987), they called for individuals to make "meaningful" observations about their contexts—in this case, their schools. Individually, students were asked to follow a research cycle that followed five steps: (a) develop community-based topics to learn more about them or seek to change them; (b) conduct primary as well as secondary research, including interviews, observations, and surveys; (c) write a traditional academic research paper; (d) produce a "real" research text (e.g., documentary, newspaper article, etc.); and (e) distribute their text to real audiences to help raise awareness about or change some aspect of their school or community (Borsheim & Petrone, 2006, p. 79). The authors spoke of the commitment, curiosity, and motivation necessary for students to see themselves as researchers who can exact "real" change in their school or community.

One interesting finding to emerge from this study was that students reported that the research project process was a positive experience, which filled the void of traditional research papers in school (lack of voice, purpose, or audience). By identifying issues and constructing research rooted in their everyday lives, the youth remained engaged in a literate process of contextualized inquiry and research. Students secured interviews with executives and political figures in their community and reported feeling like "real citizens" (p. 82). Borsheim and Petrone also wrote that many positive results were unanticipated, such as shifts in "attitudes, ownership, community involvement, and oral and written communication" (p. 82).

More recently, Phelps (2010) argued that there are uses in applying critical literacy to the nonfiction study of cultural and ideological diversity, focusing particularly on learning about Islam in America. Phelps demonstrated how critical literacy is used to debunk stereotypical and harmful representations by introducing sociopolitical dimensions. By acknowledging that the ideological foundations of knowledge, culture, and identity are always political, Phelps argued that a critical literacy lens helps to reveal the social functions of texts in positioning individuals and groups of people (p. 191). Phelps replicated Cervetti, Pardales, and Damico (2001)'s model of critical literacy that disrupted the commonplace to focus on sociopolitical issues, to develop more nuanced views on complex contemporary topics and take action to promote social justice. Citing the work of Leland, Harste, Ociepka, Lewison, and Vasquez (1999), Phelps argued that "doing critical literacy" in classrooms involves guiding learners to ask certain kinds of questions when engaging with any texts, such as: what is the purpose of the text? How does the text try to position the reader? How does the text construct reality? Whose interests are or are not served by the ideas in the text? What worldviews are or are not represented?

There is much to explore in relation to the relevance of the unanticipated outcomes in critical literacy research, including a continued interrogation of the definitions of citizenship. Janks (2010) defined critical literacy as multiple, as skill and social practice that is both embodied and shifting. She argued that there is an ongoing sociohistorical imperative for critical literacy learning that positions identity investment and the constitution of subjectivities within complex, multimodal, intertextual social spaces. She highlighted this notion of critical literacy as both a shifting skill set and embodied social practices that function through the interdependent negotiation of pedagogical domination, diversity, access, and design in various learning contexts. This notion raises the question: where can critical literacy praxis be successfully implemented?

Limitations to Critical Literacy Projects in Schools

In her foreword to Lankshear and McLaren's (1993) critical text, Maxine Greene called for a pedagogy that emphasized personal and social transformation beyond mere identification with dominant social codes. At that time, Greene (1993) contended that the postmodern emphasis on discourse, textuality, difference, and the structures of power should promote action-oriented dialogues around problems of oppression, equality, and justice. Yet time and again, postmodern scholars and their critics alike have articulated the tragic fault of critical literacy, naming the context of formal schooling as a limitation hindering social action. Although not always true, the overwhelming obstacle to critical literacy in schools has been the failure to put principle to practice and to fully enact models of critical literacy through activist actions in authentic spaces that extend outside of the classroom.

Since its entrance into educational theoretical parlance, critical literacy (like its relative critical theory) has been displaced and dislocated. It has been dismissed as being anything from too pedagogically loose a model to too politically activist a model (Freesmith, 2006; Luke & Dooley, 2007). As early as 1999, critical literacy scholars Comber and Nixon noted that literacy practices inside schools primarily function to sustain dominant cultural norms and ideologies. Even Borsheim and Petrone (2006) acknowledged that, "because of the nature of critical research, students are likely to ask questions that some people prefer they not ask about topics that some people prefer they not address" (p. 82). The focus on reflection and the examination of immediate context and internal constructions proved to be the most threatening aspect of critical literacy learning. Even when students considered sociopolitical, cultural, and ideological issues that could lead to possible action steps, they frequently did not take action if they were not explicitly supported to do so (Phelps, 2010).

In search of practical applications of critical literacy despite these critiques, Behrman (2006) conducted a review of the research on classroom practices that support critical literacy. Attempting to identify and locate teaching and learning strategies consistent with critical literacy, Behrman cited an immediate problem: critical literacy is frequently described in the research literature as a theory with practical implication rather than an instructional method. Arguably, it is both and neither. While Behrman argued that such conceptions lack consistent application, he acknowledged that critical literacy authors such as Luke (2000) have intentionally resisted the development of any narrow methodology that claimed to formulaically enact critical literacy (while nevertheless replicating certain approaches).

Citing the democratizing values of bringing critical literacy from theory into practice, Behrman catalogued a list of common practices, articulated in six broad categories for critical literacy learning tasks: (a) reading supplementary texts; (b) reading multiple texts; (c) reading from a resistant perspective; (d) producing countertexts; (e) conducting student-choice research projects; and (f) taking social action. Noting that the "social action" projects can produce unsatisfactory results despite the best intentions, Behrman found that the goals of critical literacy (detailed through an emphasis on democratization and social justice in the classroom) are not reflected in the hierarchical relations through which the classroom traditionally functions. As such, he argued that no pedagogy that presumes a hierarchical relationship possesses the capacity to fully support the development of critical literacy praxis.

This classroom-based limitation is named frequently in the research. Beck (2005) wrote in search of a "place" for critical literacy in schools. Locating critical literacy as a movement drawn out of a cultural studies tradition aimed at transforming social inequity, Beck warned against placing issues of power and difference at the foreground of classroom conversations. Connected as it is to the attitude of questioning the social, political, and economic conditions under which texts were constructed, Beck wrote that critical literacy learning involves students examining the reproduction of inequality and injustice while gaining a critical consciousness to participate in and transform their social worlds. Studying the use of critical literacy learning practices in an all-male maximum-security facility in Canada, Beck concluded that it is not a good idea to teach critical literacy in settings where silence is encouraged, such as prisons and schools.

While critical literacy has historically been theorized within classroom spaces (Comber & Simpson, 2001; McDaniel, 2006) and researched as a conceptualization of particular operations of curricula inside schools, the central purpose and function of critical literacy praxis had been articulated as an assessment of texts in order to understand, uncover, and/or alter relationships of power and domination with reach outside of formal educational contexts (Freire & Macedo, 1987; Hull, 1993; Morrell, 2004). Yet, despite being theorized as an emancipatory theory of learning, researchers have consistently demonstrated that critical literacy is limited when attempting to take social action within the context of school-based literacy curricula. This points directly to the question: where is critical literacy learning more fully realized?

In 2007, Blackburn and Clark published their collection on "literacy research for political action and social change." In it, they identified the need to take critical reading and text production outside the classroom and into activist spaces with youth to engage their immediate needs for social change through political action that is not regulated by school-based interests. The authors argued that future literacy research must engage methodologies that foreground the immediate needs of participants, particularly focused on connections between the local and the global in literacy research for political action.

Actionable Elements of Critical Literacy Praxis

Lankshear and McLaren argued two decades ago that in order to continue conducting critical literacy research, scholars need to conduct research that has historical function; approaches the process of becoming literate as more than simply becoming rational; takes an oppositional stance toward privileged groups; seeks means toward political empowerment; supports multiple literacies; and counters the essentialization of difference. The authors argued that the most serious issues confronting literacy researchers were to create and participate in studies that accounted for the subjectivity of individuals while maintaining a fight for social justice:

> We must maintain recognition of the materiality of the sign as a product of social forces and relations of power, as a lived embodiment of both oppression and possibility, subordination and emancipation; in the final analysis, we must reject any notion of the human subject which seals itself off from its own history, its own link to the community of multiple selves which surrounds it, its narratives of freedom; to construct a truly critical literacy, we need to make despair less salutary and economic, social, racial, and gender equality politically conceivable and pedagogically possible. (Lankshear & McLaren, 1993, p. 415)

Ernest Morrell is a prominent contemporary critical literacy scholar whose writing influenced my early conceptualization of this study. Morrell foregrounded his early work in a cultural studies epistemology in which the historical, social, economic, and cultural contexts of individuals and groups are explored. He approached critical literacy practice with an emphasis on situated communities where learning is defined as changing participation in relevant sociocultural activity over a period of time as one is apprenticed into activist practice.

Across his early writing, Morrell (2004, 2007, 2008) frequently posited critical literacy as a "critical theory of literacy" overtly aimed at social change. His study apprenticing youth as critical researchers of popular culture was designed around core components of critical literacy work with youth that would "capture literacy events that demonstrate academic mastery and critical consciousness" (Morrell, 2004, p. 8). In that study, he designated the tenets of critical literacy as: the ability to challenge existing power relations in texts and to produce new texts that delegitimize these relations; a consciousness of the relationship between the dominant culture's use of language, literacy, and social injustice; the ability not only to read words but to read the world into and onto texts and recognize the correlation between the word and world; and the ability to create political texts that inspire transformative action and conscious reflection.

His multiyear critical ethnography focused on the relationship between both academic and critical literacy development through participation in research for social action. The study methodologically engaged students in participatory action research in which critical social activist projects were designed with youth to create relevant, new forms of participation for them. He used sociocultural theory to approach the study of situated literacy learning with youth. He also highlighted the importance of using social theory to provide tools for the identification and analysis of hegemonic practices. Grounded in an approach to apprenticeship, Morrell's research centered on documenting the movement of a group of high school-aged urban youth from legitimate-peripheral to full participation as critical researchers of pop culture in a community of practice in which they began to see themselves as intellectuals, researchers, and social activists.

Morrell's research frequently focuses on the ways in which young people come to know and adhere to socially sanctioned ways of speaking and acting without being subsumed into oppressive relations. He argued in his 2004 study that the urban literacy classroom is an ideal context for critical literacy learning that engages students both personally and as citizens actively transforming their sociopolitical world. The findings of Morrell's (2004) critical ethnography demonstrated that critical literacy projects could produce proficiency in academic and other literacies, where student-researchers began to value popular cultural knowledge as well as academic content while developing their skills with the tools of investigation, inquiry, analysis, and text production. His project demonstrates the need for the further study of organizing projects geared toward engaging youth as "critical citizens" through critical literacy.

In Blackburn and Clark's (2007) collection, Morrell (2007) discussed critical literacy and popular culture in urban education "toward a pedagogy of access and dissent." In that essay, he contended that engaging in critical literacy involves the consumption, production, and distribution of print and new media texts by, with, and on behalf of marginalized populations in the interests of naming, exposing, and destabilizing power relations while promoting individual freedom and expression. Importantly, Morrell here wrote that critical literacy is not only necessary to understanding and navigating the language of power in dominant discourses; it is also central to the capacity to redefine the self and the social space in terms that do not replicate forms of oppression. He has noted, in the tradition of the criticalists, that the only way to come to any sort of useful consensus about the precise definition of critical literacy is to review the working definitions of the term as it has taken shape across the research. Having reviewed such work in the previous pages, I move to extend that line of thinking into the social space of urban youth organizing.

· 4 ·
STEP TWO: INTERROGATING COMPLEX PERSPECTIVES

Mapping Multiplicities

The second element in the critical literacy taxonomy involves "researching, analyzing, and interrogating multiple viewpoints" on a given issue. Multiple perspectives are key to understanding different complex positions and interpretations. This point inexorably links to the third taxonomical element explored in Chapter 6, which focuses on the identification of issues focused on sociopolitical realities. In the early stages of engaging organizing, youth may have only limited knowledge of specific issues and related social injustices. Rather, they identify issues while conducting research and seeking out multiple perspectives and continue in an iterative cycle of identifying new issues and conducting new research accordingly. All of the participants highlighted the value and importance of having safe space in which to participate and facilitate difficult dialogues.

The most prominent practices participants identified involved searching out independent, international media resources, asking questions about who owns the modes of production to control who speaks and what message is conveyed (Lankshear & McLaren, 1993). They sought out diverse perspectives on a host of issues. The pages that follow provide examples of some ways in which participants gathered sources, conducted research, gained perspective and reckoned with 21st-century information culture(s).

Vaga De Franx: Considering Multiple Viewpoints

Vaga De Franx considers complex perspectives and viewpoints through her uses of media, as well as her call for peer study groups for informal learning around books and histories. Whether interrogating the underlying messages on chauvinism or feminism, there is a way in which her habits of questioning read as a powerful form of activist decentering. In her organizing and activism, she challenges overly moralistic positions while working to include subordinate groups into her reading and her dialogues. I asked her where she got her knowledge around issues of identity and organizing. She affirmed her earlier sentiments, stating that it was through peer education and lots of recommended reading:

> VDF: I think that a lot of it has been peer knowledge. Most of it really. When I was not in Global Kids, I got all of this organizing training from other community organizations. I remember going to FIERCE and doing a workshop on race and racism within institutions. And then going to SBU [Sisters and Brothers United] in the Bronx, who did workshops on educational justice and campaign development. So I got all of this organizing training, and how great to do that. How to educate your community, how to treat each other better, what the issues are, how to teach others, and then I didn't necessarily build up my ideology…I was practicing the ideology of what was there. You know, when you work with a social justice organization, a nonprofit, even if they are not pushing an ideology on you, naturally, what you see in your community, the issues you see and why they come about and how to solve them, through the experience you start building certain values or certain ideologies of how things should be or why these things aren't working. And then you go off to college and you read Marx and you're like, "Oh, there you go." [EB & VDF laugh]. I'm living it and I didn't even know it for the past few years. So a lot of it was training, but then I read Marx, people are always surprised that I didn't read *The Communist Manifesto* until a few years ago. I read it and it makes so much sense. To me, I practiced before I even knew. A lot of it is just stuff that people recommend to me. We were talking about reform or revolution and I met people from Hunter [College] who said, "Well, you should read Rosa Luxemburg" because she talks about this issue and she talks about that issue. But you know, for example, the book that influenced me a lot over the last few

> months is called "Wobblies and Zapatistas." It is kind of a study of, a form of interview, with an activist who was a labor organizer and an anti-war organizer and warrior. And he talks about different movements in history, like the Zapatistas in Mexico and what all of these movements have in common and the ideology behind it. Like anarchism versus Marxism, you know, and class struggle and all of these things that people encounter when they organize. And he talks about how people educate each other, you know. And how the influences of organizing take place.

Here she talked about Leftist literature, history, and theory, privileging counternarratives and foregrounding ideas of difference and shared ideology. We spoke in greater detail about the multiple perspectives explored in interactive learning that happens in youth organizing workshops. In doing so, we talked about how workshops and learning function in spaces of anti-oppressive organizing with youth.

> VDF: It's funny because out of all the student organizers that I have met, everybody always says that I am the most neutral. And that I am the most non-sectarian. And I really am the least sectarian organizer that I have come across. And that is because the workshops that I learned and went through and the skills I learned from Global Kids and other organizations really allowed me to develop that patience and that understanding and that ability to break things down, to break information down, you know, to listen to experiences and analyze them. And really look past all of that theory and personalize it.

The ethical learning involved in this workshop space is striking in terms of critical literacy, mobilizing self and others as actors with skills to exercise deferral, to understand experience and to plan actions on sociopolitical issues around identity and community. I asked her for more detail about running workshops, and she named essential differences between workshops and other, more stifling forms of educating. She also highlighted crucial challenges involved in creating peaceable learning environments:

> VDF: You know, when you do a workshop, you have your audience, and you have this shitload of information that you are supposed to cram into their brains in 45 minutes. And the way of learning within workshops is completely different than learning within an institution, and completely different from just the organizing that we have been doing. But a workshop—you get in there and it's most often times a circle. You can see everybody's face and everybody is most likely looking at each other. And you give information in an interactive way. And almost in a very basic physical and entertaining

way. You don't ask your audience to list for you the number of socialist leaders in Soviet Russia. You ask them—what do they think socialism is? You know, very basic questions. And it really makes people question themselves and not get patronizing. It really means they are going along with the workshop and they are learning with everyone. And we have that safe space that allows everyone to not feel self-conscious about their lack of theory or their—how much they know. And so when I am in groups, or in meetings, I can do that with people. And we had a lot of problems because people don't know how to do that. People who are plugged in to the student movement but don't even know what safe space is. And are fighting for social justice and practicing a theory that is all about justice and equality—but yet they don't know what safe space is. And they don't realize how important it is to always implement it. So we held a workshop last week on safe space and it was the first time we had ever done that.

She went into a long aside explaining how to conduct a safe-space workshop. Vaga De Franx referenced safe space quite frequently around issues of learning and healing and talked about it in great detail across our conversations. There is a sense that she questions everyday experiences in this form of activist organizing, teaching participants to defer their judgment and seek out multiple perspectives, to not rush to conclusions. She highlighted the importance of community in this type of learning and creating a shared physical space for growth and understanding within a local organizing setting.

As we explored the connections outside of the local, I made a point of asking Vaga De Franx what she thought we had to learn from global student movements outside of the United States. She had spoken previously about movements in Chile, Quebec, Mexico, and Colombia. I asked her what she learned from international youth activists:

VDF: Definitely that, you know, being able to nationally build that national force is definitely—but in terms of legislation and government and their relationship to government is that these [international youth activist] groups have really brought up their own ideas. At this point, they're not saying this is what's wrong, fix it. They're saying this is what's wrong and this is what we want from our government and that's it. No excuses. No justifications. No asking. No pleading. No. It's come to a point where this is just not working for us, here is what we want. We are not asking. And for me, it's like – back in the fall, I remember saying at an interview, saying, or in defending Occupy Wall Street for example, "Well the reason that they make no demands is because that is not our job. Our job is to be citizens. The government's job is to come up with the solutions. And now, looking back at that, I retract completely. Because what I have learned from all of these [international] student movements is that, sometimes you can lose your faith in institutions, and justifiably so.

This critique of institutional authority resonates throughout these dialogues with Vaga De Franx. She shared experiences and observations of oppressive conditions and the struggle against apathetic and unreachable administrators at institutions of higher education. She discussed how she learned to focus efforts on direct actions and the strength involved in drafting popular information and proposals, creating shared visions with other activists. She also talked about the contradiction of institutional recognition, that acknowledgment that comes following the physical occupation of a space or similar acts of refusal. It is clear that she mobilizes student activists despite and in spite of institutions:

VDF: What happens with a lot of these student movements, and Occupy Wall Street, is that everybody thinks that it was just spontaneous. The people that were involved have been organizers for years. The people who were involved look at Occupy Wall Street as that one-year project. You know? That foreshadowed other projects. But, we see it as spontaneous and out of nowhere. But at least in the Mexican student movement, it was sparked mostly by the elections and them just being so critical of the electoral system and the corruption within the elections and within the candidates... And you have seen this amount of mobilizing and organizing of ideas and they built a student union. But they are there and they have those conditions. And later on, they are going to have to include the workers and move on to a bigger issue, or whatever it is. But, it's happening for them. And they are that critical of the state. And they become such a powerful force that, that's what we have learned here.

EB: Is that where Chile and Quebec and other student movements come in?

VDF: Yes, but even within Quebec their student union still does not include racial minorities too much. We have seen that a lot. In Chile, they haven't been able to communicate with lower-class students as well, so we've learned about that. And I think at least in New York City, the demographic is so different than these countries that we have to analyze their structures, but at the end of the day know that we need it to work for the United States and for New York City and how do we do that?

Through her connections to international organizing, she acknowledged the value of learning from other activist groups while highlighting the local differences. In doing so, she demonstrated great dexterity, moving from the macro- to the micropolitical, addressing global issues and bringing our dialogue always back to the personal.

Gentle Meadows: Perspectives on Activist Work

When we talked at first about whether or not he considered himself an activist, Gentle Meadows was quick to acknowledge the mainstream narrative that critiques (if not condemns) images and acts of activism. I asked him why he thinks people consider activism in such a negative light:

> GM: I don't think it's fruitful, but I think nowadays people think about it like—it's because society is apathetic. They think anyone who is engaging in something, that it is a bad thing. Or "It's not my business. It's completely separate from what I'm going through right now." Um, and I think that is in a way very closed-minded. And they are not seeing the big picture that everything is interconnected. And, it's noninvolvement. I feel like that's become a fad in the past. I mean I went to a very, very liberal arts school. People are very apathetic. And it's almost cool not to be an activist. Not to engage. Not to participate in your community. It's cool to just be like Thoreau and hide in the forest. Being an activist is like, engaging with people. Having a communal experience. And another thing, when I say engaging with people on a communal level, it's not just having a barbeque. It's about politicizing issues—that's definitely a big part of it. I feel like the Left, or the progressive movement in general, in the past fifty years or so has been on the defense. But a part of politicizing space is that you kind of take back—you make it more grey. That there is possibility for change, I guess that's what I mean.

Here he calls for alternate ways of envisioning and understanding activists around theories of change. His language evokes an egalitarian sensibility, that this is as much about identifying an alternate vision on activism apart from romanticized Leftist dominant discourses as identifying an alternate from the vilified corporate conservative mainstream media. He enacts this approach to alternate visioning in relation to issues of education as well as immigration. He talked in depth about studying the marginalization of immigrants in his recent research:

> GM: A huge section of my project is how these NGOs and groups function to reorient policies and ideas from a state-centric point of view to human security. So, immigration policies, instead of reinforcing the state, and having it so that it's for the state's benefit, it should primarily be first for the individual and the human being. So, instead of using immigration as a nation-building, state-building project, should be used for human rights or human welfare, human development—whatever you want to call it.

STEP TWO: INTERROGATING COMPLEX PERSPECTIVES 45

We talked about the competing narratives that inform his learning. He continued to question textual intentions and explore underlying messages as we discussed the ways in which he consumes information about current events, human rights, and social justice issues. His youthfulness and humility shined through here, as I urged him to go in-depth in discussing his news sources and the information that informs his critical perspective:

GM: I wish I knew more!
EB: (laughs) You know a lot.
GM: Like, apart from what my friends—a lot of it is from sharing with my friends on Facebook, or like social media. I don't use Twitter a lot but I've gotten a couple of things from there. Well, let's see what I have on my phone. Let's see. *Democracy Now!* is one of them. Amy Goodman, she's amazing! Um, NPR is I feel like, they could be better sometimes. They've gone way too moderate lately. I like The Real News. I think it's Canadian...I really like Rable.ca. It's Canadian. And there's another, what is it called? It's based in Montreal, I forget the name of it. Adbusters is cool too, I like them. As far as American media, I don't know. I don't know. Um, *Democracy Now!* [laughs] What else do we have? I don't even know. [long silence] But, as far as general news, I just look at *Huffington Post* if there is something sudden that *Democracy Now!* can't cover immediately. Um, but that's about it. What are other news outlets? I don't even know.

Our conversation about accessing domestic and international media and sharing information online led to a discussion of difference and relational positionality around organizing topics as he talked about the title of this study:

GM: Becoming activist. I like the fact that you use "ing." It doesn't end. It just doesn't. You keep learning about new issues and you keep on trying to—part of being an activist, I'd say, even though it is broadly defined, it's about seeing how different issues are connected to each other. And that is how you form a movement. Not just with your specific one issue. Like, for example, environmental advocacy, or environmental justice. But how that relates to feminism, for example. Or like, migrant justice. I don't know, it's a never-ending process. What does it mean? How do you become an activist?

As his rhetorical questions imply, there are many multiple ways to articulate answers to these questions. The inquiry involved in learning about various interconnected issues highlighted the use of deferral in the effort to define activist while always simultaneously growing into the term. By discussing the intersection of environmental feminism, he points to yet another way of understanding different struggles in relation to one another. This is a unifying concept that insists on remaining critical when understanding issues and dialoguing with others to come to shared platforms from which to take political and social action across local and international contexts.

Green Strawberries: International Perspectives

Together, Green Strawberries and I went into detail about alternate ways of becoming informed around issues and learning about social justice organizing. My questions related to information access, consumption, and specific sources she trusted for information:

EB: What kind of information do you consume to know all of this stuff? Right, because you don't decide to be an immigrant rights activist out of nowhere…or to understand economic injustice. How do you get yourself informed on all of this?

GS: Honestly, some of it is through books. The obvious would be the books. But I get a lot of my news from people that I know who are on the same page as me. But also, I watch a lot of South Asian news, which is so much more blunt about worldly issues as well. Literally, I don't know what channel it is honestly. It's the channel that my father watches. [laughing]

EB: It's on satellite or something?

GS: It's on the TV. It's, well, I don't know what it is. I don't turn on the TV, but my parents do. I don't watch TV, but that is the only time I will watch it. So I just tell my mom, can you put on the news. And that's where I get a lot of my news. I'll send it to you. I'll ask my mom what it is. But, the way they talk is very blunt, straight up, which is what we do not get from our media. So, I feel like I learn a lot more from that. And then *Democracy Now!* would be another thing, I listen to that a lot on the radio. Or else articles people have on their Facebook or articles that are emailed to me.

EB: Any good books stand out to you?

GS: Well, I can tell you about a book that is fiction, though, but I think really makes one conscious about a lot of things. Two books. Um, and it definitely talks about Marxism and goes into Marxist theory and all these things. One is *The Handmaid's Tale* by Margaret Atwood. You've got to read it.

EB: My mom loves Margaret Atwood.

GS: She's fucking phenomenal. And then the other one is *Caucasia* by Danzy Senna, which deals more with race. Particularly in the sixties and how that is connected in so many ways to now.

EB: In the U.S., or globally?

GS: In the U.S. And then some globally. They go into Brazil at some point.

STEP TWO: INTERROGATING COMPLEX PERSPECTIVES

Her international perspective is striking in the context of media and learning. In fact, much of what she discussed was of a global scope. When I asked about activist learning, she talked about the positions of silenced/marginalized voices—first in the context of Occupy Wall Street and then in relation to Palestine. She highlighted events and organizing strategies as she named various forms of activist learning:

> GS: I mean, when we are talking about General Assemblies—I have been to mostly Occupy Wall Street General Assemblies, that's where I've developed my view of GAs. I don't think it really works as well as—I just think they're not going about it well. I feel like I learn nothing and I get a headache after 4 hours. And I think a lot of that is because the Left has just so many different forms of what is right that no one wants to step back and say we are trying to be here for the same thing. So, I can step back a little and hear you out, but no one is willing to do that.
>
> EB: What do you think the "same thing" is? What's the common ground?
>
> GS: That they are all Left. That's it. That's really it. Then there are reformists and anarchists and social-anarchists and ISO socialists and other forms of socialists and communists and, you know, you talk to different people and it means different things even though they have the same sort of background.

Here she names the competing narratives at work within Leftist organizing and activism, highlighting their differences in ideology and their attempt at identifying unifying principles.

One topic that she named as central to her learning, her peer educating, and her art was the topic of Palestine. I asked her what made Palestine so relevant for her, and she detailed her personal commitment to activism for a free Palestine:

> GS: The fact that these days I've been recognizing how whitewashed I am. How whitewashed I have become. And trying to go back into my roots. And the Palestinians are my brothers and sisters, right. It's—what is happening to them is beyond ridiculous. So I feel like a lot of the Palestinian issues connect back, you know, to connect with my brothers and sisters in that way and their struggle and recognizing their struggle. That's why it is very important to me.
>
> EB: When you say your brothers and sisters, you're not Palestinian, are you?
>
> GS: No, I'm Pakistani and Afghani, but they're still my brothers and sisters.

She went on to talk about how frequently people assume she is white and associate her with whiteness. Her conversation foregrounded the notion of difference here, incorporating questions that explore perspectives on race and ethnicity specifically related to social and political positions of Middle Eastern and South Asian individuals. I asked her if there was ever a moment when she recognized she was becoming an activist:

> GS: Well it was around the time when I was with Global Kids. My parents are very conservative people and their views are very traditional and conservative. And being that my family is lighterskinned, they were treated as, I guess, white people in Pakistan. And so their view on a lot of issues of people of color is the same as white people. But then, they get pissed at white people. They say stuff, you know. But I was in Global Kids, and my parents didn't really let me go out and Global Kids is the only thing they really allowed me to go to because I pushed and pushed. And then one day my mom asked me, "Why are you pushing so hard? Do you have a boyfriend there or something?" And I'm like, "No, I don't have a boyfriend there." And that was around the time that I was figuring out my sexuality, so her saying that kind of offended me a lot as well for other reasons, so. But you know, literally sitting down at the moment with my mom and starting to cry and being like "How can I not?" And hearing my mom say, "What do you mean by that?" And I start bringing up issues. And she said, "But you are not darkskinned. Those are not things that you need to deal with." And I'm like, what are you talking about? I'm still a person of color and I recognize that. I mean, back then I didn't as much. But I recognize now. And I will never struggle like they do, but they are still my brothers and sisters, which is what I tell my mom. They're still my brothers and sisters. So her not getting it actually pushed me more to do it. And that was a moment when I realized I need to be doing this for so many more reasons than I thought. As a human being, I can't allow things to just happen.

People's Republic of Mars: Perspectives on Media, History, and Peace

Throughout the course of our conversation, People's Republic of Mars was quick to acknowledge policy gaps and hypocritical positions, asking hard questions about what constitutes a violation of human rights, on whose terms, and with what evidence. I turned the conversation to talk about how he consumes media to consider multiple points of view on issues. I asked him where he gets most of his information:

STEP TWO: INTERROGATING COMPLEX PERSPECTIVES   49

> PRM: Well, for me, it's from a diverse source. Like, I would do BBC, CNN, and I would compare that to, like, I would also do Fox, even though it is a little biased. But I would still be going there. For news about Middle East, I would do Al Jazeera. They have done a wonderful job covering the revolution in Egypt and everything. I just feel like it was less biased in terms of what I have seen and what I have read in other news medias. I would do *Huffington Post*. I would compare styles and just analyze the whole thing, trying to get a better picture. So, the whole different range of media. I have taken a class on literacy and public address, so I know what are some phrases that people use to make something seem more important or less important. So I feel I kind of have the ability to—I mean, no one knows what is happening on the ground, but I do research to get a better picture.

His comparative news analysis named the diversity of sources he seeks out for perspectives on current events, some of which are progressive but still major forces in the information world. Our conversation moved to the topic of bias, and we began talking about what is happening globally. He began a discussion of marginalization, examining differences in the discourses around human rights as understood in the United States and elsewhere in the world:

> PRM: I mean, for many years, our policy was one of isolation from the rest of the world. I mean, we are geographically located in a place where, you know, isolation is very favored in a sense. But now, it's a global world, you know? We cannot just isolate ourselves and not do anything about things like Rwanda or Bosnia. It's our responsibility, it's our world. You know, if someone is struggling, it will become our responsibility. But it should not be like motivated by selfish means. Like, oh we want natural resources, or a logic like that.

His call to action, to amp up human rights protection and fix the United Nations, demonstrates his motivation to create a peaceable world. We talked about summits where Third World representatives protest, but that the exercise of voting does little to change the material conditions of people in need. He critiqued the U.N., and a large discussion about peacekeeping followed. Despite critique, he argued that the "U.N. has a big role in peacekeeping and peace enforcement":

> PRM: I understand that [the peacekeepers'] loyalties should be first for their countries and second for the U.N., but kind of finding a common ground on something that, you know, we don't need like—if something like a genocide is happening, you don't need Security Council vote to try to prevent. And I feel like we should have more peace enforcement.

EB: Right. It's complicated. When I think about issues, like the peacekeepers for instance. Do you want them to have weapons? Will that promote a form of violence? I think "peace enforcement" is an interesting sort of paradoxical term. How do you enforce peace? Do you enforce it with weapons?

Awesome Woman: Speaking Exponentially

Awesome Woman offered multiple perspectives on her own work in relationship to current events and issues she organizes around locally. In doing so, she considers multiple viewpoints and alternate ways of seeing social, political, and cultural topics. To speak exponentially on local and global subjects, she reads deeply:

AW: So, I like to read a lot of blogs. Like, Saddam Hussein's ex-mistress. And she is—well that's what she is famous for. Or, that's how I got to know her. But she writes all about racial tensions within the Black community, and history, and she writes a lot of novels also. She's kind of just like a Renaissance woman.

EB: Is she in the U.S., or is she—

AW: She's in the U.S. And so I follow a lot of people. So media, I dive into that. Also, I just have like—because I've been in all these different diversity trainings. And so I have a lot of texts. But, I'm really about reading traditional—well, not traditional. But the issues I am involved with, sort of like the bibles of these different topics. So like…

EB: So like…authors?

AW: Yeah. Like Audre Lorde is super important in that way. About being queer, or being Black and queer. Or being of color. And, I started to read "Gender Outlaw." I'm not finished with it.

EB: Kate Bornstein?

AW: Yeah. I met her! Oh my god. She's such a character. I met her at this, like this femmes conference. [laughing] Yeah, that was really interesting. Yeah, so I'm reading the bibles. And I'm really interested in Richard Wright, and, in general, I'm also interested in spirituality and how that manifests in different contexts.…So, I've read the Bible sometimes. I can't read the Qur'an for some reason. I'm going to learn how to read Arabic next semester so that I can really read Arabic and—so yeah. Those are kind of my sources and just like, I watch a lot of stuff. Things that are thrown out to me, I do watch. Yeah, so I put myself out there for information. So, not—I'm taking stuff in, but I also put it back out there. And I don't really say anything rude, you know. But I still say, like, I have an audience for some stuff.

STEP TWO: INTERROGATING COMPLEX PERSPECTIVES 51

At one point in our discussions, I asked her why she engages in activism around specific issues, specifically looking at issues related to women and to religion:

> AW: Um, so—why do I do that? So, I feel like right now what I organize are things that are more like cultural programming. All of them are not necessarily acts of activism, but they can be. Like I'm on the board for the Islamic Student Association at my school. Usually, it's kind of like we're meeting together and we share a similar spirituality. But when things happen—like for instance when the NYPD surveilled us, like we're on that big list of schools—I took a big part in organizing our teach-in. And that's when it becomes activism. When you organize, when you have this community, you keep it strong and whenever a threat comes to this community is when it comes to activism. Organizing in general can be about that community and when you have an issue that arises, that is when it becomes activism.

In talking about these moments where cultural and personal issues become overtly politicized, Awesome Woman articulates ways in which she responds to moments of injustice, bigotry, and hatred. She highlights her responsive output to inputs she receives:

> AW: I feel that my personal activisms are more about educating people. So, I get angry a lot. I made a video one time and—well no one would say, or some people would say—that the video was like, me being an activist. But, essentially it's not very obvious. So there were a couple of people on Facebook talking shit about women's bodies. Like, "summertime is coming, I better not see your jelly rolls." And blah blah blah. And, "Ladies, you can wear one pieces." And I'm just like—that's not your body! Why do you have an issue with someone else's body? And that pissed me off because that further perpetuates the negative images we have of women's bodies. And we just allow that to happen. And it's just like, who are you, man, to tell me what to wear? And who are you to say anything about my body? And I feel like a lot of people have these negative—a lot of people are really uncomfortable with their bodies at all. There are so many body issues. And it's like constantly we are being slapped in the face with it. And people say this is what we're supposed to look like. But not—we're humans and we're supposed to look like a whole bunch of different shapes and sizes. People don't know that. So I made a video and basically what I said was if you don't like it, look away. That's what it was about. But I did outline why it is like that, why you can't do that, and why you should stop doing that. So, for me, that was an act of personal activism. And some people took it in and were like, you have a point. And it really isn't for me. I really have no reason to say what a woman should wear. So, the person who was really

	adamant about this. When they saw the video, they messaged me and they were like "you're right." And I was like, snap!
EB:	That's the goal, though, right? Some kind of education?
AW:	Yeah. Education is super important to me and just in general—so I don't let a lot of stuff slip by. People always think or say "oh you're easily irritated or agitated" and I'm like "No! You're just an asshole and I tell you why you're an asshole." [EB laughs] I'm not going to let you continue to be that way because that's just not who I am. My mission on earth is not to let people just continue being how they are. I feel like I have to say something. I just can't sit back and let things slide by. If no one says anything to you, you're just going to keep doing that, saying that to other people and making other people feel like crap. And who knows what that one little comment can do to a person.

· 5 ·

ORGANIZING A SPACE FOR JUSTICE

Tracing Definitions of Activism and Organizing

Recent youth organizing work is expanding the idea of young people engaging in activism. Activism here is understood as one key component to cultural, political, and social movements (Reed, 1981), in relation to which individuals further develop their sociopolitical identities (Watts & Guessous, 2006). By undertaking social activist projects, social justice-oriented youth organizers reframe ideas about civic engagement to consider how power informs civic and community life. In the process, they foster their abilities to understand, question, and challenge the subtle relationships among their identities, cultures, and politics (Ginwright, 2010b).

In what follows, the context of youth organizing is introduced as a community-based space from within which critical literacy learning takes place. This involves many challenges: first, to define the terms of youth organizing and activism through a poststructuralist approach to question and defer signification; second, to delineate something of a nonnarrative, nonexhaustive history of past and present activist organizing projects; and third, to trace the reach and limitations of youth organizing projects to establish the need for the present study.

Describing Divergent Histories of Youth Organizing

Youth organizing is a relatively new field of research, a hybrid space that is activist in content and that actively resists cooptation. Obviously, youth engaging in community organizing and social activism have a long history well before either concept was even considered a "field" for study. Broadly speaking, the contemporary study of youth organizing is an extension of positive youth development, situated in the crux among traditional youth development, youth leadership, and community organizing.

Various approaches to youth organizing work have come out of an integration of community organizing principles (Alinsky, 1971; Reed, 1981) and critical pedagogy (Freire, 1970) into the field of youth development (Camino & Zeldin, 2002; McLaughlin, 2000; Mokwena et al., 1999). While there is no single definition or model for organizing and activist projects, the process of engaging in social justice-based community organizing can generally be understood as a collective response to forms of political, economic, social, and cultural forms of marginalization. In youth organizing contexts, young people are conceived of as agents of, not subjects to, change (Ginwright 2010a). They have rights and skills to exercise in the present as they take on roles of community leadership.

As an identifiable group, youth organizers are defined in relation to the work they do to alter unjust and inequitable landscapes by mobilizing campaigns and actions around human rights, social justice, and democratic citizenship. The specific features of youth organizing include many functions that could be simultaneously understood as critically literate practices, such as: (a) the cultivation of habits of community-based participation through (b) the development of a critical consciousness in contexts where youth (c) talk explicitly about their identities and focus on (d) leadership development through (e) civic and literacy skill building such as critical thinking, creative problemsolving, public speaking, collaborative planning, critical text production, and group dynamics (Warren, Mira, & Nikundiwe, 2008).

Youth organize around topics such as employment and labor rights, healthy food, climate justice, educational justice, police brutality, homelessness, and poverty. Of course, not all the youth involved in such projects are poor or workers, have been brutalized, or have experienced educational neglect. By crossing borders of communities with their peers and adult allies, youth organizers frequently explore topics that are historically unaddressed (or even avoided) in schools, from class identities and sexual orientation to immigration status and the operations of local governance. As research shows, youth organizing projects promote the most authentic approaches to systemic change on the youth engagement continuum (see Heinz, 2012). The notion of the authentic here is significant; organizing builds around the self-defined priorities in the lives of the youth themselves.

Positive Practices of Organizing

The study of youth organizing and activism emerged out of the field of youth development, built on a foundation of an analysis of power and inequity. In organizing programs, such processes are learned through the practice and acquisition of skills necessary to pursue policy and social change, from lobbying and campaigning to taking direct action (Yee, 2008). Predominant conceptualizations of youth organizing have come out of an integration of community organizing principles into positive youth leadership programming (Clary & Rhodes, 2006; Delgado, 2002; Flanagan, Syversten, & Wray-Lake, 2007), and community development initiatives (Irby, Feber, Pittman, Tolman, & Yohalem, 2001). Proponents of positive youth development (PYD) came to agree on three basic tenets of youth organizing: society must have a vision for its youth, who grow up in communities (not programs), and thus youth development must address the overall social and political contexts in which development occurs (Ginwright, 2010a). Whereas PYD focuses primarily on the individual, youth organizing places the emphasis on both individual development and social change, where youth work collectively to understand their personal struggles in broader social and political contexts.

Across this multifaceted sector of research, scholars and organizers have forwarded various models of community-based youth work dedicated to civic engagement and social action, purposefully designing organizing programs that respect the intelligences, leadership abilities, and passions of young people (LISTEN, 2003). Such social action projects are focused on youth political empowerment (James & McGillicudy, 2001) and civic engagement (Flanagan & Faison, 2001). Prior efforts to research youth organizing have focused on identifying components of models that could be used for replication (Flanagan, Syvertsen, & Wray-Lake, 2007; Warren, Mira, & Nikundiwe, 2008). These studies use critical research frameworks, merging studies of youth community action with sociocultural factors such as youth popular culture (Gonzalez, Rodriguez, & Rodrigez-Munez, 2006), antiracist identities (O'Donoghue, 2006), issue-based campaigns and civic activism (Sherrod, 2006; Torre & Fine, 2006).

As current research demonstrates, youth activists are guided by concepts of participatory democracy and the inclusive awareness of all willing participants within the complex principles and values of social justice (Ardizonne, 2007; Gordon, 2010). This social justice-oriented activist approach to youth leadership and citizenship development offers the learning space for youth to recognize injustice and act on it (Sherrod, 2006). Youth organizing focuses on a direct model for civic action, where action is understood as collaborative, public activities for desired change. Assessing promising models of youth organizing, Ginwright (2010b) called for the development of linkages between and amongst individual, neighborhood, and community member initiatives in the interest of promoting broader democratic engagement while fostering positive social development.

Watts and Guessous (2006) argued that a focus on the sociopolitical development of adolescents is overwhelmingly absent from research on youth development, citing the risk that nonprofit and governmental organizations face being charged with political indoctrination and antinationalist sentiments. In particular, certain forms of democratic citizenship and advocacy work with youth are seen as too radical. Yet, as Morrell (2007) wrote, youth-initiated critical research can serve as a potent tool for advocacy and positive social change in urban contexts. Durand and Lykes (2006) call youth organizing a space that moves from a youth development model of empowerment to one of genuine social solidarity with youth, supporting them in the development of skills to actively advocate, organize, and mobilize on their own behalf and on behalf of their communities.

One noteworthy organization conducting research on the current state of youth organizing is the Funders Collaborative on Youth Organizing (FCYO), a collective of researchers, grantmakers, and organizing practitioners. In 2010, the FCYO conducted a comprehensive survey of youth organizing groups operating across the United States, producing a field scan report that identified 160 organizations in which adults and youth work collaboratively to create opportunities for community organizing and advocacy (Torres-Fleming, Valdes, & Pillai, 2010). A substantial majority of these youth organizing projects focused on urban youth of color and operated within the nonprofit youth development sector. While this sector is not the only context for youth social action and political participation, it suggests that a sustainable space exists for refining future models of youth organizing (HoSang, 2003).

Contextualizing Urban Youth Organizing

Social justice-oriented youth organizing is focused on an intentional exploration of the relationship between young people and grassroots community change, placing issues of justice and equity at the center of youth development work (Ginwright, 2003). In particular, working in urban settings, youth organizing projects address the intersection of race, economics, and geography. They forward an integrated approach to social change that combines issue-based organizing, trainings, and actions with leadership development, political education, and social movement histories. Young people in urban contexts often have to negotiate higher concentrations of poverty, disappearing jobs, underfunded schools, and a lack of clean public spaces (Kincheloe, 2006).

Organizing projects provide a rare opportunity for urban youth to consider their rights as adolescents in a democratic society and to take social action to redress injustice and inequity (Ginwright, Noguera, & Cammarota, 2006). Urban educational researcher Anyon (2005) argued for a specific focus on urban youth in the development of sustainable activism and organizing projects. Pointing to the centrality of young people in civil and economic rights struggles historically, Anyon identified the need for public social spaces outside of schools to do this work with youth.

Over the past two decades, urban youth organizing has emerged in educational research as scholars have begun to focus on spaces of learning and positive youth development outside of school. Today, many community-based organizations in urban contexts engage young people in activism around problems defined by the youth themselves. In the process of organizing, they teach critical techniques for research and outreach through social and political activist campaigning. Alongside innovative forms of youth development and popular political education, youth organizing projects have increasingly become incorporated into community-based work with urban youth.

Across the existing literature on the positive implications for sociopolitical identity development, urban youth have reported that participation in organizing projects contributed to them beginning to value themselves as social and political actors (Ardizzone, 2007; Lewis-Charp, Yu, & Soukamneuth,

2006; Sherrod, 2006). Leading youth organizing scholars have demonstrated that when urban youth identify needs in their communities and articulate their collaborative vision for social change, they utilize literacy skills and analytic tools that foster critical perspectives which result in a greater sense of civic responsibility (Ginwright, 2003; Haj & Abu, 2009; Warren, Mira, & Nikundiwe, 2008).

Conducting Activist Research with Urban Youth

The 2011 report from FCYO presented some of the most comprehensive mixed-method, large-scale research to date on the impacts of youth organizing across the United States (Shah, 2011). Amongst some of its most significant findings, the report showed that involvement in organizing projects helped young people "become engaged in the civic and political life of their communities" through the development of "critical social analysis" skills; this in turn led to a growing sense of agency, "through the belief that they have control over their actions and can make a difference in the world around them" through civic and political action (Shah 2011, p. 11).

Researchers have demonstrated that youth organizing is an exemplar space for youth leadership development by training youth to mentor, peer educate, conduct research, and create critical texts for social action (Delgado & Staples, 2008). Youth organizing holds the potential to serve as an exemplar space for urban youth leadership development, forwarding an advanced form of leadership training in which youth are supported to be ethical decision-makers and capacity building community leaders. In a study of urban youth activists engaging in struggles around issues of language privilege, youth voice, and social justice, Ardizonne (2007) wrote that youth reported that their motivation to participate in various social and political action projects within community-based youth development organizations was that they felt they were supported as growing activists, collaboratively involved in the direction, content, and purpose of their learning, while affirming their ability to use their voices and actions to design campaigns and projects.

After conducting qualitative case studies of youth in community organizing contexts, O'Donoghue (2006) concluded that community-based organizations can build organizational intentionality around literacy, youth voice, public language, participation in decisionmaking, skills development, and public projects that provide structured opportunities for youth-driven social and political organizing initiatives. Through the processive skills and practices of organizing, youth activists refine their tools and practices for reflexive social and political action. Sherrod (2006) has called for further research and advocacy to explore the role of civic engagement to promote social justice and human rights learning within youth activist projects.

Argument Around Literacy in Organizing

Morrell (2004) argued that urban youth, often constrained within academic literacy practices at schools, are uniquely positioned to enact critical literacy praxis outside of school in organizing contexts. Some common pedagogical components of youth organizing projects include generative issue development; consensus building; critical media inquiry; community research; political analysis; policy advocacy; protest; direct action; and reflection (Lewis-Charp, Yu, & Soukamneuth, 2006). While these components have not been explicitly identified in relation to the study of literacy, literature on youth organizing consistently demonstrates that youth activists engage in forms of critically literate praxis through continual processes of ideological inquiry, critique, and strategic social action (Ginwright & Cammarota, 2007; Larson & Hansen, 2005).

In some ways, this work in youth organizing points toward the necessity of developing a politics and pedagogy of voice that opens up texts to a wider range of meanings and interpretations while simultaneously constructing student experience as part of a broader discourse of critical citizenship and democracy. Lewis-Charp, Yu, and Soukamneuth (2006) addressed the implications of youth organizing and activism in the development of positive identity formations among urban youth. Their research stated that "critical self-awareness not only helps an individual identify the seeds of her own problems, but also sheds light on dominant discourses that contribute to her marginalization and oppression of others" (p. 23). Such practices point toward the critical reflection of the self as community member and activist, building an understanding of oneself and others in the pursuit of social and economic justices.

As if in answer to the challenge of conducting critical literacy learning inside school spaces, the field of youth organizing is an exemplar alternative space for critical literacy to be enacted outside of schools. These spaces support youth engagement in activism as a process to make social and political change (Strobel, Osberg, & McLaughlin, 2006). In many ways, such activism aligns to the working conceptions of critical literacy praxis. By intentionally taking critical reading and text production outside of the classroom and into activist spaces with youth, organizing engages the immediate through direct social and political action (Blackburn & Clark, 2007).

· 6 ·

STEP THREE: IDENTIFYING SOCIOPOLITICAL ISSUES

The third element in the critical literacy taxonomy involves identifying issues focused on sociopolitical realities in the context of the lives of the learners. This section is slightly more condensed because of the connection to the previous and following taxonomical elements. Such an identification of issues involves conducting research on multiple perspectives, designing and executing actions around those issues, and reflecting upon the steps taken. The social and political are central to the operation of critical literacy as well as to the work of youth organizers (Ginwright, 2010a). I use the work of Watts and Guessous (2006) here to define the sociopolitical in relation to understanding agency and opportunity structured around civic service and social justice. Sherrod (2006) pushed this idea further, rooting the sociopolitical in the sphere of urban youth activism. This focus on identifying sociopolitical issues in the context of the communities in which learners live is fundamentally the work of critical pedagogy and popular political educational models.

Vaga De Franx: Focusing on the Sociopolitical

For Vaga De Franx, her activist work is grounded in her commitment to community. She talked about emphasizing the social element of activism to understand the connections between the personal and the political. In particular, she highlighted the importance of focusing on the social and the political when organizing around any activist issue:

> VDF: I guess the one thing that for me makes you an activist is being active in your community or society. But there has to be a political reason or a social justice reason for you to do what you are doing. So, if you become a vegetarian because you personally want to be healthy, that might not necessarily be an activist thing to do. Whereas, if you become a vegetarian because you believe that the meat industry or the way that our society produces or overproduces meat, or in third world countries how there isn't a large supply of food, then even though that's a personal choice, to me that is activism to a certain extent...You're doing it consciously for a political or social reason that is not for your benefit alone. Now, I guess that to me that is what makes you an activist. But then there is also—is it just you becoming a vegetarian or is it part of a larger, you know, movement where people are planning on going vegetarian together. I think that there are different levels of activism, but to me as long as you are doing it for a political or social cause, and you're conscious of that, then you're being active and you're an activist.

She understands the connections across and between identities and ideologies in her discussion of organizing social movements around political issues. She explains the role of theory and practice in her current work organizing and discusses the choice of her student activist group to remaining politically unaffiliated:

> EB: Where does ideology fit into actual radical struggle and practice?
>
> VDF: I think that has always been an issue with movements. How do you move from theory to practice? And I think, like *Wobblies and Zapatistas*, what you see now is revisiting that theory and—especially with anarchism and socialism, which is what it argues—anarchism is all about practice, and socialism is all about theory, but putting theory into practice. But you've never seen societies actually reach communist or even the ideal socialist society. So building that bridge, I think, is extremely useful. Choosing to remain—because everyone has the right political line—so choosing to remain and be a student group that doesn't have a set political line, that has kept us from being sectarian in many ways. But at the same time, there are things that are socialist in nature in theory and we are really learning a balance, even within our structure. We have centralization, we have core people, we have representatives that have one vote, or two votes. We have consensus, because consensus is set so that everybody has to agree.

> We have votes. Those representatives have to represent their campuses, you know. But we still have campus autonomy, so each campus can do what they need without having to come back to a central committee or something.

I asked her to talk more about her thoughts on local action as she reflected on the work she does now and the work she will continue into the future. I was curious about her sense of accomplishment and success related to local projects, and if she envisioned herself continuing to organize around the issues she engages with now. I asked if her focus on education is a result of her position as a student and if she thinks she will move on to other issues:

> VDF: No. You know, I think that I'm always going to be involved in education because students are always going to be in a pivotal role. That's not just because I'm in that age group and we're pivotal. They've always been pivotal. And they've always—you can't keep them isolated. It has to be accessible to everyone, education. You know, even as a worker, if I were to move on and become a worker or a mother or whatever, it still affects me. If we're talking about saving public education, and rebuilding it, and really making it public, then it's an education that is going to be accessible to the community. It's not just about resources, but it's about being able to make decisions about it. Having community spaces. Having the university serve as that. It's going to be important, whether I'm a worker or a senior citizen. It's something that hasn't changed at all. So I'm always going to be tied to education. It is just such a vital part of our society, especially higher education, I can't see myself as not being a part of that.

She challenges power and the language of power in her discussion about making demands around issues locally, and her focus on higher education highlighted a complex tension around institutional agitation, acknowledgment, and silencing. Much of our conversation, as well as my observations of her activism, related to reports and experiences of injustice within the university setting.

Gentle Meadows: Reading the Sociopolitical

As he related ideas of activism across issues, Gentle Meadows shared his understanding of the connection between personal and political through the notion of "community-based politicization." I asked him to explain how people politicize issues:

GM: I would say conversation, discourse. That's the—a lot of people would say that it's not fruitful or it's not good for change. But, by talking about something, people rethink what they previously thought. It's not taken for granted anymore. So that questioning that happens in your head, it brings up the idea that, oh, maybe there are other possibilities out there, not just the ones I have known all my life. Or that I have been taught in school by a different generation. So, it's a catalyst for change, definitely.

He identified the value of competing dialogue and narratives as he highlighted the ways in which multiple perspectives on a given issue can challenge one to reposition themselves vis-à-vis social and political topics. It brought us to a conversation that looked closer at his history as an activist, and I asked him how he got involved in this work:

GM: I think Global Kids. That's the only, or one of the only things that really gave me this social justice bent. Like, I was part of Model United Nations in high school, but that was more focused on debate and your speaking skills. And, you know, your ability to back information up with specific examples. And it's not, it has nothing to do with—it is personal gain. It is all about you controlling the stage for thirty seconds, or one minute, or however much time that you have. So, you simulate how government bodies work. And, I mean, it's good to get young people thinking about how they would react in like high levels of government. But at the same time, Global Kids—it has a very grassroots level that is very close and personal. That is more easily relatable definitely. And just the different workshops. I mean, it's not just—it's not the banking method. Like in classrooms in U.S. history or European history. You actually do workshops, you play different games and that is how we used to start our activities. And then you act it out, you do it with other people, collaboration is emphasized. And I feel like today education has become lonely, solitary, sedentary. Even when you are doing homework, it is just you on your own. So Global Kids, the type of learning and how learning happens is very interactive, and interpersonal. I feel like not only do you retain more that way, but it also teaches you that—maybe it requires that I work with other people to succeed in life. And it's not just about you doing everything on your own.

So much of Gentle Meadows's power lies in his calm fearlessness, positioning himself in ways to continually rewrite ideas and redesign actions as he learns more. His discussion about critical security studies brought us to a conversation about queering the performance of security and the concept of state power as a form of constructed identity:

STEP THREE: IDENTIFYING SOCIOPOLITICAL ISSUES   65

EB: It's interesting when you reference Butler. She was one of the formative people when I started studying queer theory. Just to have her come off the tongue, to use her name and know what it means. I don't come across that very often.

GM: Yeah, it's interesting. I remember one article, it was Cynthia Weber I think—I don't know if I'm pronouncing that right. It was about how the state's identity is constructed. How it's a performance, and she uses Butler to perform her analysis. I thought it was interesting. I buy it. A lot of people in the class didn't. Even in a liberal arts school like mine. Surprisingly.

EB: Well, I buy it, too [laughing]. So, why do you buy it?

GM: God, well, I need to look at the specifics of the article. But, I mean… So constructivism, it's all about identity and how identity influences your actions, or if it's not a person, the state. And how you can predict what a state would do. And it has to do with how others perceive you, so in the community of states, different relations are constructed by different things. So it's not all about military power and who has the most weapons. Or who has the strongest economy, so it's also about language—human rights language, human rights talk, discourse—that constructs one's identity, it's not just physical, tangible things, like guns or military capabilities.

This was important because the conclusions I had begun to draw about this study pointed to a queer theory of activism, in which youth organizers gather around issues that foreground difference in an effort to provide just and equitable spaces for learning.

Green Strawberries: Roots of the Personal in the Political

Green Strawberries has strong connections to the issues she organizes around. She is very personal about her politics, and her passion comes out assertively when she talks about issues of human rights, justice, and equality. Her focus on the sociopolitical first emerged through her understanding of the connection between the personal and the political:

EB: Okay, so break it down. What kind of organizing do you do?

GS: I've mainly focused on—and this is just—I don't know why—but on immigration. Undocumented immigration and student rights have been my main focus.

EB: You don't know why?

GS: Well, part of it has to do with having family that are immigrants, um, South Asian and South Asians here are mostly immigrants. And then I

	got involved with this organization called D.R.U.M.: Desis Rising Up and Moving, which got me really into immigration policy and law. And that's really where it started. And being that my best friend is undocumented, and having her go through so much, there was no way that I couldn't—I would have had to do something.
EB:	What about student issues? What kind of issues?
GS:	When it comes to upper-level education, mostly tuition and stuff like that. When it comes to high school and middle school, it's more about what kind of education they are getting and how they are being treated. The policing in these schools. Those are the issues I deal with.

She explores power relations and challenges systems of institutional oppression. In doing so, she seeks to attend to those she perceives as silenced. It is noticeable that she always includes subordinate groups in her discussion, whether youth or racial, ethnic or sexual minorities. The definition of subordinate is shifting here, as she demonstrates in her discussion of LGBTQ rights. She measures power and cultural capital to determine which issues to devote her time to and which to not focus on as intensely.

EB:	When we were talking in Union Square that one day, we talked a lot about gender rights and LGBT topics, too. Are you still involved in that kind of organizing in queer communities?
GS:	Definitely, definitely. But not as much, only because I feel like the LGBTQ community has grown so quickly in power than any other. If you really think about the history, I mean the U.S. history, of the LGBTQ activism and organizing, it really happened in the sixties and it just keeps going. And it's because anyone can be LGBTQ. It doesn't matter what race, what class. It could be anybody. And I think that as time goes by, we start to recognize how fluid sexuality is—it's just becoming such a powerful community. So, in that sense, I haven't really been doing as much because they are already doing so much. So, if I can give my time to something that is doing less well—you know.

People's Republic of Mars: Challenging Power Relations

People's Republic of Mars is deeply knowledgeable about issues surrounding international diplomacy and the conflicting perspectives around the operations of the U.N. Army. He talks about the corruption and duplicity of ambassadors in various locales in the world, and he highlights the need for meaningful work that affects subordinated groups for public good. As he spoke about the connection between the personal and political, he began to detail the various activist work he engages in:

> PRM: I was inspired by HRAP to create my organization. And, right now, we have two schools. I mean, we will be—it wouldn't be fair if I said I'm not doing anything. I'm doing stuff, but it's not me directly doing it. I'm making perhaps, like helping people do it. But that is also considered kind of activism. So I think that is why I started the organization. I volunteer time. A lot of my friends have their own nonprofits or their own initiatives, and I go volunteer here and there.

He talked about his experience volunteering at various initiatives, revisiting and complicating his original definition of activism as action on the ground. He also talked about the ways in which he uses language to challenge positions and postures of power:

> EB: So, I've read a lot doing this research and talked to a lot of people about the critique of rights, which is a fairly interesting thing to think about. Like, that the U.N. or the U.S. or anybody involved in the creation of the UDHR—that those were first-world countries with first-world interests. Do you ever confront that?

He went on a long aside, talking about the Universal Declaration of Human Rights and the concept of human rights generally as a "good framework." He discussed the divides between theory and practice and accentuated the point that there is always bias in implementation. He critiqued the bias in various religions that promotes forms of condemnation instead of tolerance. Talking about human rights policy, he highlighted the disjoint between foreign policy initiatives and consistent implementation:

> PRM: But, I mean, whatever the documents that we have right now, they are good. They just—the implementation is biased. For example, even like U.S. in general. They would not be forcing countries to implement human rights the same way. You know, Saudi Arabia, for example. We never worry about who is running the country, what kind of rights are there and what kind of rights are respected. But we would be voicing our opinions and concern over Iran, or some other country that we are not good friends with right now. So, I feel like the implementation is very biased.

His critique of the bias in human rights protections in practice brought immediately to my mind the nearly twenty-year gap between *Brown v. Board of Education* and the forced integration of segregated schools in the United States. Our discussion included much emphasis on subordinate groups and ways to provide for the politicized articulation of counter-narratives and self-determination amongst such groups. He focused in particular on immigration policy and the struggle of undocumented persons:

> PRM: Like, DREAM Act—I love my work with immigration. When I was in high school, a lot of my friends, even though they were talented, they were super talented, all the grades were very good, everything under their belt, but they couldn't go to good schools because of their immigration status even though they lived here their whole lives. You know? So, I am always active whenever something comes up. Like, when a recent update happens. For instance, recently Obama kind of, like, was suspending the deportation of young undocumented immigrants who would have been benefited from the DREAM Act. So, just updating people about things like that. You know, that's just—the DREAM Act is something that I want to see passed. So that's something I feel like I would do more work on. Just, try to like—not only DREAM Act. Just to get comprehensive mediation. I think that DREAM Act should be, would be a first step. But work to make sure that there is comprehensive immigration reform passed.

Awesome Woman: The F Word

Awesome Woman's tendency to drift in and out of story is a key part of her ability to peer educate. She is at turns macro and micro, enraged and joyful. I learned so much in simple conversation with her. She discusses difference by foregrounding feminism, accentuating the connection between the personal and the political across issues. In our conversations, she constantly crossed borders of identity, exploring the tensions between social rigidity and moralistic position taking. I asked her when she first began her activism, and she told me a story that was highly personal and detailed in its remembrance. I excerpt here at length to highlight her nuanced memory:

> AW: I can say I started to be an activist when I went to Sudan for the third time. I went to school there, for almost a year, I went for a whole school year.
> EB: How old were you?
> AW: I was eleven. No, I was twelve, and I turned thirteen then. My birthday happened while I was there. And I remember, like, I was terrified to go to school. Um, or I was optimistic, but I was also terrified.

STEP THREE: IDENTIFYING SOCIOPOLITICAL ISSUES   69

EB: You had been here?
AW: Yeah, I was coming from a New York City school, post-9/11, coming from a really shitty experience. Like even after Sudan, when I came back for 8th grade, awful experience. But I'm glad it happened, because I don't know who I'd be. It made me an optimist. So bad! The worst times of my lives, really, and I just remember in 6th grade being bullied like crazy, out of hand, but I couldn't even tell the teacher because then you would be a snitch. And nobody respects a snitch. Like, it was dangerous. I couldn't be me, and I couldn't even say anything really. Because I know my dad, he is the kind of guy that is like "I don't care what the laws are, I'm going to protect you." And I was like, I can't have my dad being crazy. You know what I mean, that's a big deal. And if I told, then what would happen to me? You know, there were just a whole bunch of things going on with that. And I remember coming to—going to the Sudan, and I'm just like, wow, kids are going to accept me because they are like me. No. I was American as fuck to them. But I was like, I was a foreigner terrorist here, but when I came to Sudan it was like, you are American, you represent evil.
EB: Wow.
AW: Yeah, and I felt that. I really felt that.
EB: That's crazy.
AW: Yeah. And my classmates—all my classmates were international rich kids. Some of them are coming from parts of Europe, and they are either Sudanese or, like, other forms of Arab. Or, there was also an Asian girl, one Asian girl. Their parents were either in business, or government, which is also business, or they are just rich in Sudan. And so, and also, I am poor in America—I think I'm poor—but in Sudan, I do have money there. So, I'm just coming from this very interesting background. Coming here and I just expected them to be open with all arms. But no. It was very difficult. I remember being in fights every day. I never had a fight in my life in America. And now, I had so many fights. Like, every day I would fight girls. I went to an all-girls school, all-girls Islamic school. All-girls Islamic international school. Big deal, it was like—so much. And I remember, so okay—one time, I had a friend. So what happened was, eventually, all the English-speaking kids, all the foreign kids who were not from Europe or did not speak Arabic, formed a pact. So I had friends, I had a friend from Florida whose parents—and she was like me in a lot of ways and she is from the U.S., her parents are also both not Sunnis. Her mom is African-American and her dad is Sudanese. My mom is Haitian, my dad is Sudanese. So I was like, "Oh my God, twins." [laughs] I had another friend and she was an Egyptian-Irish person. It was like "Oh my god, you're Irish and Egyptian." She looked one way but talks and you're like [AW makes surprised look on her face]. And she was so different from me. And I had another friend from Canada. But Mada [pseudonym] is the most important. She was my—I remember when I was really sad, um, she—because she got promoted to another grade, just because her dad was like, "I'm

going to give you money, promote my daughter." And I failed the English exam—no wait, I failed the math exam, so I got left back technically. So I was in 6th grade. But—so she bit a teacher. And that was because—so you are allowed to hit kids, in that school. And so, I witnessed it, so when he was trying to hit her, he brushed up against her. And I don't know if it was on purpose or not, but she bit him because of it. And she got in trouble because she bit him. And I was like, "Yo, this is not right. Like, I can't—this is totally not right. He like, molested her or some shit, I'm not gonna." So, I remember I was crying because, I was like, my friend is going to be expelled, like my one really tight friend, and we had this similar background, and I loved her, I couldn't let this happen. So I was crying and crying, and she was sent to the principal's office. And people were saying rumors like "Oh, she's going to get in trouble" or "they're going to expel her" or whatever. So, one time, in class, the same teacher is talking and he was like "she's a troublemaker," or whatever, and so I ran to the principal's office—and the principal is also my distant relative, and I went down and I screamed "He..."—and you know, I was very embarrassed about body parts too, but no—he touched her boob. You can't let that happen. He definitely did. And that's why she bit him. She has a right. She felt like she was being attacked and she attacked him back. And people were surprised. Because I don't—I never really spoke up about anything except, I used to just fight. That was more like fighting then and I never got in trouble because my aunt was like headmistress, but still things were difficult for me. And I also didn't tell anyone that she was my aunt, and I would go to the headmistress but not get in trouble. And I didn't want to say anything, and she didn't say anything either. And I was just like "No, this is not okay." I think that is what I can identify as my first act of activism.

EB: It's incredible.

AW: Yeah [laughing]. I—I was crying, saying like "No, you can't do that." But yeah, that was it. The first act of activism and that came from a really—from a place of me feeling like the cultures I was a part of were very womenhating. And I really wanted—I really felt a lot of anger about that. And so, coming back to America, I definitely really became more active about it. But that is what I think of as my first—yeah.

As she detailed that story from her youth and traced her activist history as a feminist and a Muslim, she discussed her most recent trip to South Africa. In the process of interweaving this retelling, she leveraged the silenced/marginalized voices of those she knows, those she meets, and all who are oppressed:

AW: I'm trying to think of, like, really profound moments on my trip. There was one time, when I was on this bus with this kid who, like, I don't think—he told me I was the first Muslim person he spoke to. This was a white

STEP THREE: IDENTIFYING SOCIOPOLITICAL ISSUES 71

>
> Afrikaner kid. We spent—we were going to a national park, and we spent like four hours on a bus together. And I'm not sure what's his experience with Black people or women. And we had an intense conversation about religion. And he was talking about Christianity from his point of view, which was so interesting to me because I asked, "What sect are you?" And he said, "I don't have a sect." And I'm like, okay, but the things that you are talking about are very specific, versus, like, the Christianity that I am used to, which is like—because he was talking about, or really his main argument with me was about that he thinks that Islam, that some of the things that we require Muslims to do is performance. And he was trying to define performance for me. His English, also, wasn't the best. He was trying to explain performance to me, and I was not getting it. I was actually kind of offended. I was like, what do you mean, performance?

EB: Like, Judith Butler, or no?
AW: [laughs] Yeah.
EB: But not?
AW: Well, performance. And he was talking about how, that to be a good Christian, all you have to do is believe there is a God. And I was like, what you don't have to pray, you don't have to go to church, you don't have to be a good person? You don't have to give charity? Or what? What does it mean to be a good Christian? And I was just thinking about it, and I'm like, I wonder what his context of Christianity, tied to South Africa, how does he get that? And then I was thinking about, in general, what were the people who came to South Africa here for? They came on a mission, right, but when they used Christianity as a means to it, I'm like, what are their ideas of what a good Christian is? And how is that translating down to this fellow? Like, what that means. Because basically he was saying, "If you're chillin', you're a good Christian." And I'm like, there's more to it, I'm sure! I don't know. I don't use him as the example of what Christianity is, because I have had so many sources.

Awesome Woman went on a long aside about experiences with the other U.S.-based students who traveled to South Africa with her. She highlighted the need to be inclusive and open to understanding multiple perspectives to get a sense of what is so politically and emotionally charged about social and cultural histories and memories:

AW: I feel like if you really bring folks together and let them talk, they will realize. Like the conversation I had with the guy. He was like, "whoa, Islam is the same thing as Christianity, basically." And I'm like, "I knew that." But to him, it was some foreign thing where we are just dark people and—you know.
EB: That's a challenge for you, I'm sure. You know some stuff, and you have to educate people whether you are in South Africa or Brooklyn.

AW: Yeah. And that's always a challenge too because sometimes I feel like, is it my duty to educate everyone?

EB: It gets exhausting, right?

AW: It gets so exhausting. I'm just—I need to stop telling people about myself. You need to research. Like, I can't be the Rosetta Stone of Otherness for you [laughs].

EB: You're not trying to be a native informant, bell hooks style.

AW: Right, I am not trying to do that. But I do believe in educating people as is possible in informal ways. So that's a challenge. But the guy that I was talking to, he was saying all of these things to me, but then he was like, "Can I be honest with you? This is the first time that I had a real conversation with a black girl. Like a black person period." And then later, toward the end of the trip, I was getting really tired and it was late at night, still on this bus, I was trying to get comfortable, and he was like "Do you want to lean on my shoulder?" And I was like, what the fuck? This dude asked me to like—and in my mind, maybe I'm making it bigger than it is—but in my understanding of his context, this is the first time that this is ever going to happen for him. When he tries to engage people in the future, what does it mean? And so, I was thinking about, I sometimes have conversations with people and I don't realize how epic they are until later in life.

EB: You're pretty epic.

AW: [laughs] Thank you. But things like that, I'm just like—every conversation in South Africa was pretty epic on its own.

· 7 ·

DESIGNING ETHICAL RESEARCH

Theoretical Framing of the Study Design

Primarily, this research is presented as a qualitative interview study with five urban youth organizers. I selected the specific participants because of their diverse commitments within the context of youth human rights activism in and around New York City. As I researched and worked to bridge the social and political with a focus on literacy, I engaged the participants in reflexive dialogue around the forces that pushed them to become personally and politically activist in the multiple cultural communities and issues in their lives.

The goals of this data collection and analysis were four-fold: first, to explore how urban youth organizers engage in critical literacy praxis in their activism and organizing; second, to examine how urban youth organizers articulate their identities as they become activists; third, to consider the implications that the various articulations of participants may have in the further study of youth organizing as an innovative out-of-school space for critical literacy praxis; and perhaps most importantly, to facilitate a dialogue around organizing with activists, educators, and researchers that contributes to greater connectivity and collectivity. In the pages that follow, I describe the theoretical framework for conducting this study. I move to detail methods for selecting participants, approaches and limitations to collecting data, methods for analyzing the findings, and some considerations of research validity.

Conducting Ethical-Political Research

Identifying urban youth organizing as the backdrop for this work, it is important to foreground the contention that urban issues are worthy of study by urban youth themselves. The practical application of critical literacy praxis within urban activist spaces allows youth to purposefully negotiate contested authority and construct positive identities, possessing the potential to effect social change. Whether dubbed presumptuous or activist to do so, I took on this study in part to see how this research can support further training of youth activists and organizers with the intertextual tools to engage in the war of ideas against hubris, xenophobic prejudice, and anti-intellectualism. This is important when thinking about research through a cultural studies epistemology in which to "open up spaces for authentic dialogue, new forms of participation, and curricular projects that are immediately relevant to the lives of urban youth" (Morrell, 2004, p. 12).

Ethical-political research respects divergences and does not seek to essentialize participants into easily identifiable categories that treat subjects as objects in need of external diagnosis. "Ethical-political strategy" is a concept that has been applied to much critical social scientific research when foregrounding the subjectivity of research participants in respect for their self-reportage (see Behring, 2013). Patti Lather, a leading postfoundational educational researcher, defined the "ethical-political" as that which does not dictate moral and political propriety but rather seeks to understand the impetus behind such prescriptive dictates (Lather, 2001).

Thus, to conduct DKPNYC as ethical-political research, it was important to conceptualize a methodological plan of study created through and reflected upon in dialogue with participants as experts of their own experience. Since critical literacy is understood in relation to its deferral of definition and youth organizing is a space resistant to academic cooptation, this study is well suited for the consideration and application of methods that do no moralistic harm to the subjects of study.

Following Lather (2001), there is a centrality of praxis, of "research as process," through a critical emancipatory model of reflexivity. This involves a level of what Lather called "undecidability," a reminder "that moral and political responsibility can only occur in the not knowing, in the not being sure" (Lather, 2001, p. 187). Thus the emergent design of this study was greatly influenced by the individual participants. This model of emergent design allowed for research relationships to be developed and sustained through continuous reflexive dialogue on becoming activists, engaging a process built on collaboration that resonates well beyond the parameters of the research agenda.

In turn, this research project was conceived of as an approach to collaborative and participatory research that provided participants with opportunities to refine research and interview questions, to determine methods of data collection, analysis, explication, and representation of findings (Cammarota & Fine, 2008). It is an appropriate approach in part because the topics of human rights and social justice take seriously ethical questions. In what follows, I outline my role as researcher in negotiation with the multiple subjects of study before moving to discuss specific methods for data collection and analysis.

Polyvocal Subjectivity and Role as Researcher

As primary investigator, I aim to be transparent about my bias and my subjectivity. The reason for this is because I defer to the subjectivity of participants; I see my role as researcher as an exploratory one into communities of learners, looking at civic engagement, youth development, and social justice organizing in order to add support to anti-oppressive struggles alongside youth. I believe it is valuable that these youth engage in human rights activist and social justice organizing, and I seek to understand how and why they do so. Thus this research was designed, in part, to offer a space for the participants to engage in critical reflection, considering their identities as activists and further positioning themselves as agents of social and political power. This support calls from across the educational research landscape for social scientific inquiries into youth leadership that is connected to critical civic engagement in out-of-school spaces (see Ginwright & Cammarota, 2007).

Such designs add to understanding about the constitution of subjectivity, looking at the ways in which youth organizers articulate their activist identities as they engage in critical literacy praxis. By working in participatory ways with study participants, I sought to provide a forum for research that simultaneously allowed these youth activists to broadcast their positions and their multiple messages, to counternarrate, peereducate, and connect with others involved in the same, yet always different struggles through a polyvocal approach to a politics of difference (Giroux, 2005). Hatch (2002) has characterized such attempts toward polyvocal educational inquiry as an intimation toward poststructuralist research, where research is designed with the contention that truths are multiple, fragmented, temporal, and contextual. Undertaking a polyvocal approach involves a series of steps that include: identifying all contributing voices, writing a narrative of each selected voice, refining the narrative and revising to best represent each included voice (Hatch, 2002).

The design herein thus forwarded research that is strategically ethical-political in its reportage of the multiplicity of youth activist voices, understanding the diverse experiences of urban youth organizing through the organizers themselves. While qualitative research may traditionally tend toward a more holistic interpretive analysis, intentionally polyvocal research moves beyond the phenomenological goal of ascertaining "the meaning," "the structure," or "the essence" of the experience of participants (Tobin & Davidson, 1990). Polyvocal research considers the various meanings, structures, and constructions of experience and offers alternate modes of representing findings. Thus, the write-up of the study reflects the multiple meanings participants make of their experiences while simultaneously analyzing their critically literate praxis as activists. Below, I outline the emergent research design structure and discuss the actualization of that design in negotiation with participants. I first address sources for data collection and end by discussing steps of analysis.

Research Setting and Participants

The study focused exclusively on a small sample of urban youth activists who were all participants of Global Kids' Human Rights Activist Project (HRAP) when they were in high school and who are still involved in activist projects at their colleges and/or in their communities. The Human Rights Activist Project is the youth organizing component of Global Kids (GK), a community-based nonprofit organization in New York City. HRAP is a program that fuses social action techniques with GK's approach to positive youth development, supporting youth to lead human rights campaigns that impact policy while equipping them with tools to become lifelong community leaders and activists. HRAP thus provides the historical background from within which this study emerged.

There are numerous other youth organizing projects operating in this city and other urban areas in the Northeast (see Ishihara, 2007; Shah, 2011). I chose HRAP due to my personal experiences as an educator and facilitator in the program, where I observed youth engaging in critical learning while designing social action campaigns. Following Ginwright's (2010b) poststructural ethnography, I aimed to interrogate youth organizing as personal and biographically specific (for both participants and researcher) while challenging assumptions around the essence of easy identifications as activist.

The diversity of participants in HRAP made it an ideal program for sampling a range of activist alumni from across demographic groups. Broadly speaking, the youth who participate in HRAP are racially, ethnically, and socioeconomically diverse. The majority of participants come from New York City neighborhoods and ethnic groups that are largely underrepresented at American universities and in many professional spheres. The majority of participants in the program identify themselves as African American, Latino, South Asian, Middle Eastern, East Asian, or Caribbean, and most attend schools with poor attendance and low graduation rates, in underserved and politically marginalized communities (Global Kids, 2011).

The participant sample was selected purposefully to include youth who could understand what Hatch (2002) called the "transformative intent" of research designed to encourage political action. Purposeful sampling is common in qualitative research as researchers push back against the notion of a "representative sample" of any group in favor of selection based on criteria—such as shared characteristics, settings, or activities (Maxwell, 2005; Patton, 1990). While purposeful sampling evokes criticism as lacking objectivity, it can serve to capture heterogeneity in context.

The particular sample of participants I drew are individuals who were all members of HRAP when they were in public high schools in NYC and thus have that shared historical-organizational context from which to speak about their past, present, and future instantiations of activism. Specific participants were selected through a process of snowball sampling (Patton, 1990) to access a diverse sample of individuals by ethnicity, race, gender, sexual orientation, and religion—reflecting at least a fragmentary cross-section of urban youth activists in the United States (Shah, 2011). In order to map the articulation of themselves as activists through the critically literate praxis of organizing, this study designed and employed the qualitative data collection methods detailed below.

Data Collection

In the initial design of this study, I aimed to conduct "critical auto/ethnographic research" with these youth organizers (Anderson & Irvine, 1993). Ethnographically, I designed this research to incorporate interviews, observations, and artifacts to study activist culture. Due to limitations of access and proximity described in detail below, the study was restricted to qualitative interviews. Although not the original design, it matches the caveat of "emergent design," which acknowledged that there could be shifts in the collection of data in negotiation with the participants of the study. Interviews serve as a potent match for my "critical auto/ethnographic" overture of working alongside youth to have them self-reflectively report their personal experience in connection to wider meaning.

To understand the positions of these urban youth organizers as activists, data were collected predominantly through qualitative interview (Rubin & Rubin, 2005; Seidman, 2006). Qualitative research with interviews serves to uncover the meaning that subjects ascribe to the structure of their experiences and their perspectives (Hatch, 2002). These interviews achieve the multiple outcomes Lincoln and Guba (1985) maintained could be elicited through qualitative research questions: participants explain their motivations and activities in past and present events, self-reporting their emotional and intellectual responses to activist literacies by reconstructing memories, constructing experiences, and projecting futurity.

Interviews began upon IRB approval and continued throughout 2012. Each interview was semistructured with ethnographic questions that were descriptive, structural, and contrasting in order to explore emergent themes. The interviews were informal and dialogically responsive to the input of participants. On average, these conversations were approximately sixty to ninety minutes in length and covered a host of themes around activist learning and organizing. Each interview was audio recorded and transcribed to identify how to further investigate and analyze emergent themes in depth in future interviews. Following thorough transcription, the audio data were destroyed. Subsequent interview protocols were drafted upon analysis of the first round of interview answers to generatively extend our dialogue based on participant input and organically emergent topics. Over time, I expected that participants would become better at talking in more sophisticated forms about their experiences. With recognition that the researcher is the primary tool of research in qualitative research, I expected, too, that I would become better at listening to the participants as the study developed and answers emerged.

Description of Data Analysis

Out of respect for the subjects of research, data were analyzed and coded in cooperation with participants to ensure that criteria for analysis were not overly prescriptive. Creating conclusions in conversation with stakeholders allowed for an important reflective critique. In doing so, participants could further identify, explore, and articulate their positions, their learning, and their needs. To do so, participants collaborated throughout the process of research, setting the terms for collecting data and pointing to emergent themes for analysis and conclusion. Despite the shifting outcomes from the emergent design, the final product included hybrid principles of critical discourse analysis (Rogers 2004; Rogers et al., 2005).

Critical discourse analysis is an effective approach to analyzing these data because it employs a social theory in which discourse constructs, represents, and becomes represented by the social world (Fairclough, 1989; Fairclough & Wodak, 1997). Attempting to answer questions about relations among language, identity, and society, critical discourse analysis emphasizes meaning-making as dialectic, socially constructed, interactional, and always situated culturally and historically. Thus, critical discourse analysis can be used as more than a tool of critique, bringing together micro- and macro-analyses of social and political forces. Further, this method of analysis demands reflexivity from the researcher (Chouliaraki & Fairclough, 1999), acknowledging the processive nature of (de)constructing meaning around the subjects of the study. Van Dijk (2001) called for critical discourse analysis to take hybrid approaches so as not to authoritatively delimit the experiences and perspectives of participants.

As such, this study hybridizes discourse analysis through Foucault. I take my working definition of discourse from Foucault (1972), who wrote that systems of power, made up of practices, simultaneously offer the space to liberate and constrain subjects. Discussing the parameters of discourse, Foucault (1972) named discursive spaces as the locales from which truth and falsehood are produced and made pertinent. He argued that this space is characterized by the interplay between "a code which rules ways of doing things…and a production of true discourses which serve to found, justify, and provide a reason for these ways of doing things" (Foucault, 1981, p. 8). This conception is useful in studying the discursive space of youth organizing, where the discourse of activism and organizing is simultaneously outlined and interrogated by asking questions about what is thinkable, speakable, and doable in these contexts.

Process of Data Analysis

The following steps were undertaken in order to systematically organize, review, unpack, and analyze the discourse of the youths. Each of the youth organizers was examined in detail. An analysis of each interview was conducted through the taxonomy of critical literacy praxis (Comber & Simpson, 2001; Lewison, Flint, & Van Sluys, 2002). I organize the language of the participants into five categories in order to code their articulated discourse: (a) mobilizing self as social actor to disrupt the commonplace; (b) conducting research, analysis, and interrogation of multiple viewpoints on an issue; (c) identifying issues focused on sociopolitical realities; (d) designing and undertaking actions focused on social justice outside the classroom; and (e) reflecting upon actions taken and creating vision(s) for future project(s). An initial reading of the data through this framework provided insight into understanding how the elements of critical literacy praxis operate in the subjects' activisms, identifying examples of each element as retold through the language of the participants. This analysis served to organize clusters of trajectories for emergent themes and lines of inquiry pursued in subsequent rereading.

Activism and activists are defined in relation to their engagement in events that are unique to their historical-material moment. Bringing a polyvocal understanding to the ways in which youth organizers articulate definitions of activism and interactions with the texts and contexts of activism provided visions of themselves as activists. I searched the collected data for examples of the participants using the term "activist." Of course, spoken identification is not the only mode through which to align and position one's self within the realm of activism. Still, these moments in the transcribed text provided essential examples of self-definition, defining activism and the self in relation to that definition. In the end, research questions are answered with the understanding that these (and all) young people are continually becoming, that answers change as sociopolitical contexts do.

Limitations to the DKPNYC Study

There are many limitations to this study. The initial design as "critical auto/ethnographic" was proposed to ensure that this research allowed participants many levels of polyvocality. Conducting observation and artifact analysis aligned with ethnographic overtures toward triangulation in order to strengthen the claims of research reporting (Hatch, 2002). Although I initially worked with participants to plan observations of them in workshops, trainings, and campaign development sessions, there were limits to my ability to observe them in their organizing space.

The primary obstacle to conducting observations was related to access. Most of the events in which they organized were in secure spaces within universities and/or within the homes of specific individuals. I spent more time with Vaga De Franx in public organizing spaces than with any other participant. Gentle Meadows was outside of the city for much of the study, participating in activist pursuits in the context of closed-door shareholder spaces. People's Republic of Mars went abroad and thus was limited to dialoguing when he was occasionally in New York. Awesome Woman and Green Strawberries were deeply involved in the back channels of organizing, going to undisclosed locations with small groups to organize social justice actions.

As qualitative interviews emerged as the primary data source, analysis of artifacts in the context of activist observation became less necessary. The interviews served as a powerful retelling and reconstruction of the experiences of activist work, providing insight to answer the research questions. Dialoguing around approaches to literacy learning and articulations of activism produced rich data for polyvocal write-ups of each participant. While early stages of this design posited these write-ups as "portraits," social scientific portraiture as designed by Lawrence-Lightfoot and Davis (1997) lacked the political force to allow for necessarily fragmented stories to be told without gestalt essentialization. Instead, findings are drafted in narrative excerpts that highlight critical literacy practices.

Transgressive Validity

To attend to the question of social scientific validity and to accommodate the wide variety of responses and interactions with the youth participants, analysis was conducted with participants throughout the course of the study. Each interview transcript was sent to the participant so that he or she could reread for emergent themes, propose and identify trajectories for further inquiry, and clarify any errors or vague details. After conducting both stages of analysis, participants received a digital copy of all of my write-up. I answered any questions participants had about my analysis via email and in person. This process continued until all data sets were thoroughly analyzed. These steps were taken to ensure that member checking supported the findings of this report (Hatch, 2002). Further, the representational design of the findings was meant to produce the greatest amount of polyvocality and transparency possible, recognizing the limits of coauthoring through pseudonymity.

As such, I use forms of Lather's (2007) catalytic and transgressive validity to position findings into some illuminating (if intentionally inconclusive) implications. Lather's own work serves as an example of new directions in qualitative research, and I attempt to follow her path in resisting the commodification of study (see Lather & Smithies, 1997). Lather's approach to validity in educational research is connected to ongoing questions about reportage of findings, of how to ethically represent the many truths of other people in writing beyond representation. Lather approaches validity through discourse, citing Britzman's (1991) contention that discourse "words the world." Considering validity in and as a presupposed site of methodological authority, Lather offers a counterpractice of "transgressive validity" that "foregrounds the insufficiencies of language," "gestures toward the problematics of representation," "fosters difference and heterogeneity," "supplements and exceeds the stable and the permanent," "embodies a situated, partial, positioned, explicit tentativeness," and "brings ethics and epistemology together" (Lather, 2007, p. 128–129).

The lack of finality and conclusivity in such an approach does not, however, negate the truth of the self-engendered articulation of the participants. The final product of study meets Hatch's (2002) characterization of poststructuralist research as that which reports polyvocal truths through multiple voices. In the end, this is a text that represents the multiplicity of ways that urban youth organizers engage in critical literacy praxis as they articulate themselves as activists. Beyond that, the proof is in the people.

· 8 ·

STEP FOUR: TAKING SOCIAL JUSTICE ACTION

Activist Action in Organizing

This chapter introduces the fourth element of critical literacy: designing and undertaking action focused on social justice outside the classroom. This chapter is the most exciting in terms of the "active" elements of activism and organizing—the "doing" of "being" activist. Here, the participants provide remembrances and reconstructions of some dynamic activist projects they have undertaken so far. It is here that the work of activism is most explicitly outlined in real time through the words of the participants. Historically, much youth social activist work was begun inside schools but geared toward social and political audiences outside schools (Knoblauch & Brannon, 1993). It is noteworthy that such work was frequently challenged at the level of school administration and superintendence. The crux of this study is thus focused on ways in which activist action is supported and undertaken outside structures of formal education.

Vaga De Franx: Taking Action

The bulk of my exchanges with Vaga De Franx were related to the topic of action. She spoke in our first interview about positioning herself and her learning within the context of youth development organizations. This related to her understanding of ideology and deciding to participate in certain forms of direct action. GK and other youth organizations had taught her to consider her point of view, "how to relate to the community, what is community, you know all of these ways of relating to everyone and working on these issues in a holistic way." She suggested that the world of community-based organizations did not tend to be too politically adventurous or daring: "But it was so good. I can do what I do now because of that, you know." She's been working with more overtly political student groups since then. In identifying these varied levels of activism, she tapped into emergent themes around engaging in social action within institutions of higher education. On her current organizing and activism, she said:

> VDF: I think it is the most adventurous and most exciting work that I have done…It really is self-organizing and the fact that we are doing it without salaries or a boss or—it's literally us—it gives it a sense of accountability. It is far more; it is stronger to me in that setting. Just seeing the way that students work within institutions like the university has been such a learning experience for me.

She demonstrated a commitment to activism that makes it seem as though she has always been doing this work. She talked about the movement from spectator to actor not only for herself but for those working around her in Occupy Wall Street and the free university movement. She noted that even when a social movement shifts or changes, the power and skills developed can be taken forward and reinvented in other locales. She provided a snapshot of one particular friend of hers. He had only recently joined up with Occupy before the NYPD shut down Zuccotti Park:

> VDF: And one of the things I've always thought was, once an activist, always an activist. You know? You can't just turn off that button. And now that he does not have Zuccotti Park, he can't go back to there, but he has something that now he just can't let go of. And now he is organizing on campus, and now we're building that sense of community. And everybody is doing that, you know. Occupy Brooklyn, Occupy Baruch, Occupy the Bronx, you know. At the same time, the way that Occupy Wall Street unified labor unions, community organizations, it also built this other group of people who have never been active like this. And now, we have those people plugging back into those communities and joining up with these organizations, and helping these organizations. And, to me what is amazing

is that Occupy has helped these organizations and these organizations have helped Occupy. There is a feeding off of each other type of thing and if there is a big encounter, it is going to happen and it is going to be huge and people are going to see that what they are doing locally is going to come together and show something. So I'm not too worried. People are really worried and disappointed, kind of just like "Is it dead? Is it gone?" But I think that in the years of organizing that I've done, it doesn't worry me too much. I feel like there is a natural process of organizing. It's very organic in a way. People are going back to their communities, organizing there, and naturally they are going to want that big encounter...whatever it is, we are going to need that because we all need the reassurance that if you plan a big protest, everyone is going to show up in solidarity.

There is a deep sense of reflection in Vaga De Franx about the goals of community building. In the process of planning and participating in actions, from sit-ins to teach-ins and rallies, she changes the existing discourse around her. She talked about her experience with "Bloombergville" at City Hall, where she camped out on and off for three weeks during the summer of 2011. She discussed it as a counterspace from which to position herself, a vantage from which to initially respond to Bloomberg's budget cuts.

The main forms of organizing that went on at Bloombergville were through general assemblies and consensus-based decisionmaking: "It was basically like a mini-Occupy because we were smaller in numbers and the media blackout made it like we did not even exist. Bloomberg started to evict us, and he did so easily." Shortly thereafter, Adbusters released the call to Occupy Wall Street that went viral across the Internet. Vaga De Franx talks about this distinction. She remembers the feeling that there was a personal connection with Bloombergville versus the form of Internet-based organizing in the nascent days of Occupy:

> VDF: So we would make decisions based on how to handle food, how to handle security, how to handle all of these things—but as far as demands, we couldn't make decisions on where we were going to go, or what demands we needed to solidify, because we did not know how many people were going to show up.

September 17 arrived and Occupy set off. Working groups were put in place to take care of the aspects of gathering services and supplies. General assemblies took over as the main organizing tool: "Even organizing a general assembly of that scale was something that we figured out in the process." She equated this balance to the essential questions of reform or revolution, planning or spontaneity. "Occupy was a weird hybrid of both," she said of Occupy's embrace of competing narratives and creation of public counterspaces. She highlighted the complexity of horizontal organizing within a massive economic and social justice movement, where, by definition, a multiplicity of relevant issues defies any guise of unification. She went on to talk about critiques of Occupy and her vision for future organizing actions.

Gentle Meadows: Taking Action

Gentle Meadows acknowledged that he was not as involved in forms of direct action in college as he had been in high school. He did have a lot to say about the movement for college endowments to divest from fossil fuel companies and to invest in socially just investment, demonstrating the way in which his activist perspective had shifted:

GM: Another thing that I am really conflicted about, even my friends too in college, is—so it's the SRIC. Socially Responsible Investing Committee. So it's, I am really conflicted about it because I don't know if it is radical enough to create significant change, but I was a part of it.

EB: So explain what it was.

GM: So it's investment advocacy, it's shareholder advocacy. So using the endowments of colleges to pursue political and social goals. So, for example, we work with an NGO called the Responsible Endowments Coalition. They're based in the city, and they pretty much get around to many universities—maybe 40 across the country—and try to get their endowments to pursue different things like environmental sustainability, campaigns against—when Citizens United, what's the term for that?

EB: Plutocracy?

GM: Campaign finance reform. Or like, my college, what they did a couple of years ago, was stop—this is super minor, but it's why I am so conflicted about it, even though I'm not a part of it anymore—stop McDonald's from using a pesticide. But things like that don't change power relations.

EB: They don't change power relations, you said?

GM: Yeah, like material existence…I mean, yeah you get them to stop using a particular pesticide, but at the same time, they switch to a different kind. So I don't know how effective that is. But, I mean, that's been effective like in the 90s, during—or in the 80s, I'm getting my decades confused [laughs]—but South Africa, Apartheid, a lot of universities divested from South Africa and joined the movement. And that's one way that kind of advocacy accomplishes. There are different campaigns. A lot of other

STEP FOUR: TAKING SOCIAL JUSTICE ACTION 87

	schools, I actually met people from the University of Pittsburgh at the conference.
EB:	Oh really? Cool.
GM:	Yeah, they were part of that. I don't know if they are—if they are the people, or the university leading this, but I remember them talking to me about how they were interested in using their endowment for, um, to stop or get companies to change from mountaintop removal practices. Yeah, so a lot of issues came up. Like, we talked to the Board of Trustees. They are very conservative, even at my liberal college. Some of them are flat out racist and say these really ridiculous things, even at a super liberal arts school. But anyway, like, they—we wanted to divest from a lot of companies… Um, well for example, they are invested in a lot of unethical companies. Like [companies] involved in producing weapons for Israel… Like, what are other ones? A lot of unethical pharmaceutical companies that my liberal college has invested in. And a lot of colleges are invested in these companies just for making money.

Divestment and socially responsible investing has had a recent resurgence through renewed campaigns to fight climate change. Gentle Meadows explained to me the function that students played in advocating around endowment divestment:

GM:	So our job only consists of suggesting possibilities for them to consider. And most of them get rejected if it's too controversial or too radical or if it's not going to make the college any money. I mean, I guess it's a fact that green companies or ethical companies don't make as much money as other ones, but I mean, I don't know. So, another thing that they advise us to do, instead of divesting, which was something they we're really against unless there was a really big movement like what happened in South Africa, was share out or what is it called? They have all of these technical names for everything. Anyway, so what happens is you submit a proposal to a company saying, "Hey, you should change or reconsider your policy" on a given issue, like pesticides. And they would reconsider it and have a shareholder vote in their meeting. And like for example, as our college, we have a vote in that. Out of like thousands of people. I mean, it's not a lot and it would probably fail, but, if they don't reconsider that, it goes to the media or at least the media have an opportunity to cover it [laughs]. Given that our media is biased now [continues laughing]. And they would get bad publicity, but that's the worst thing that can happen to them. So I don't know how effective shareholder advocacy can be.
EB:	It's interesting listening to you talk about them voting. Because when you showed up tonight, you were talking about whether or not you were going to vote in the upcoming presidential election.

GM: Yeah, yeah it's true. I don't know how active voting can be. It could change things but it's not progressive enough I don't think. For systematic change, I don't think voting is—yeah. I don't know.

In multiple ways, Gentle Meadows challenges the power of institutional structures as well as the symbolic act of voting around economic interests in higher education. In the same community, operating from the same locale but with a different vantage point, he talked about the other community-based work he does as a literacy volunteer:

EB: So then, maybe talk a little bit about the topics that are closest to you. What are you organized around?

GM: Um, on campus, in college, I'd say primarily I worked with other issues that maybe are more secondary to me. But off campus, in the surrounding neighborhoods—for example undocumented youth and the access they have to education. That's huge for me. And a lot of students from my high school were undocumented. Even though it was unspoken and no one really talked about it, there was this unspoken understanding that yes, there was a certain population that—really a huge portion of our school is undocumented. But anyway, so for three years in college, I volunteered at this project where you teach and tutor adults, adolescents, and children in the Hudson Valley in the English language. Just like in high school, it's not communicated to you that they are undocumented, but you know at least some of them are. And I thought that it was really important. And while not everyone in the program thought of themselves as an activist, I definitely think that they are doing activist work. I mean, I try to make it interactive. But sometimes with just two hours a couple of times a week, it's hard to get them to learn a lot of things with the time that they are given. I don't know, I don't know what else to say about it. It's really rewarding but it's hard too. There's definitely not only a language barrier, but there's also a racial barrier, there's a—there's this gap because you are a different sexual orientation than them. There's a, I mean, I don't come from a rich, or even a middle-class family, but there is really a class divide. These people would probably be earning less than poverty levels. And the fact that they are undocumented and that I have legal documents—that's another divide that I would say are divides we need to close by providing access to education and other methods. So, that's one issue.

This connects back to the sociopolitical in many important ways. His discussion of adult education training as a form of activism unpacked numerous class- and identity-based issues under the umbrella of literacy.

In his current moves as an activist, we returned to talk of the online nature of organizing. I told him that many of my interviews for this study focused on the nature of activist learning online. I asked him if he thought analog or digital organizing was more effective:

> GM: Um, I mean I like both equally. I do have a preference for physical mobilization, but online networks and online communities are awesome, too. Um, I mean. I don't know what to say about that. Like, yeah, so I sat in on this one class. It was an anthropology class on media. And like different—what online communities mean and how it differs from real-life, in-person engagement.

Across our conversations, it was clear that many of his activist pursuits are fundamentally about discourse, challenging and changing existing discourses around issues of justice and access to information:

> GM: I mean, I support the Bradley Manning case. Like, just like what he said in his testimony, information should be free. And I think that is activism. Releasing information and even like creating information. Like documenting what is going on on the ground from your perspective as a person, as a bystander, that's definitely activism I would say, even though, even if the person doing it might not consider themself an activist.

In his pursuits, he creates opportunities for engagement with subordinate groups while studying the relationships between power and language to understand relationships between personal experience and larger cultural stories. A major point here is that taking action is not always about physicality. There is much to explore in the intellectual, digital, and community-based study of the relationships among individuals, information, sociopolitical issues, and activist organizing.

Green Strawberries: Taking Action

When it comes to taking a position, (re)writing, and designing her way into a world of activism and organizing, Green Strawberries has much to say about the role of art as a form of creative response:

> EB: What about producing? I know that the one time we were talking about doing what my writer friend Katie Byrum calls it "Kamikaze Poetry." Leaving art in different places. Do you feel like, are you involved in the production of information? Or, you know, are you making anything these days?
>
> GS: I've been doing a lot of street art lately. It's mostly about Palestine and Israel. Students and immigration and all that stuff. And by the way, when

EB: I talk about immigration, I'm not talking just about U.S. immigration. I'm talking about Palestine for example, so it's broader. But I have been doing mostly a lot of street art…A lot of my work, it's mostly spray paint. And I usually do a background that is very random. Whatever inspires me at that moment. And then I stencil in whatever writing, or words, see sometimes it's just a word, like freedom.

EB: Right. You make your own stencils?

GS: No I don't make my own stencils. I have before but… I do have, I'm doing this with someone else too. And occasionally that other person will work with me. So, but not always. So, you know. For certain reasons, for safety reasons she can't always be with me. We do have an image that we go by. And when I do something independently, it's a certain letter. And when she is doing something independently, it's under another letter, but with the same logo.

EB: Do you have photos of any of your stuff?

GS: No I don't. Never.

Her movement from spectator to actor is noticeable. In particular, she focuses on the real "work" of activist organizing—meeting and planning, as compared to the aggrandized notion of activism distilled down to the singular image of the shouting protester.

EB: Right. So we have talked a bit recently and you had been at Irving Place and these different places—so where have you been recently? You've got some stuff going on!

GS: [laughs] Recently, it's been more meetings than anything else, but I can't really talk about it because it is some action that is going to happen. So it's private, but is going to be very radical.

EB: But then will it become public in its moment?

GS: Yes.

EB: Okay, I got you.

GS: Um, there is going to be this huge thing where the cops will get involved and people will probably get arrested. That's pretty much what we are dealing with right now, and it has to do with immigration policy and whatnot. So mostly, literally, it's been meetings. That's what I have been doing lately.

Here, she lays down the importance of preparation in organizing, holding teach-ins and meetings, interrogating policy initiatives and planning strategic actions. In the process, she acts to educate and change the existing discourses around her on the topics of immigration and education. Action is understood for her as much in organizing processes as in any one moment of outrage or protest.

People's Republic of Mars: Taking Action

When we spoke about taking action, it was in terms of designing actions and positioning People's Republic of Mars in relation to his past and current activism and advocacy:

> PRM: Activism doesn't have to be like, just standing in front of something and chanting slogans. It could be just changing something that's not—that you do not perceive it as being right. You know, that could be poverty; that could be just making sure that people get the education that they deserve... It could be a single thing like that. Just like, feeding people. I work in a soup kitchen. All of these things would be considered activism.

I wondered if the other participants would agree with this definition, as well as absolutists on the topic of activism. Is it moralistic to stand up against something you perceive as not right? And what does it look like to "change" poverty or hunger in practice? Is feeding people a form of ethical activism? I wanted to know more and asked him how he became an activist. He immediately named Global Kids and HRAP:

> PRM: HRAP was a big part. HRAP started—or planted the seeds of activism in me. I would be working on the DREAM Act, I would be working on anti-discrimination, so many different things. Food justice. I got involved with anything, pretty much. That's the beginning. That's the start.

Although he didn't go into great detail about his initial motivation to get involved, he was highlighting a form of intersubjectivity. He noted that he wasn't doing as much activism as he had previously, that he was more involved on organizational and policy levels:

> PRM: So, I am not currently doing like, ground activism right now, but I have done that before in the past. I feel like I am still involved in activism. Just telling people what is going on in the world and what they should be doing about it is a form of activism.

Awesome Woman: Taking Action

For Awesome Woman, an important part of her activist work involves her creation and dissemination of original information, programming, and educative materials. In particular, she uses media to actively challenge inequitable power relations. She spoke on multiple occasions about her use of video:

> AW: Another video I made was about the question, "Where are you from?" And it talked about, like, geography versus the essence of where are you from? I was really mad and I made it like two hours after an incident happened. Like, it happened and I went home and I was like, I'm going to video this.
> EB: That's such a good exercise, such a creative way to respond.
> AW: So yeah, I constantly disrupt the commonplace because I just have a lot to talk about. Like one thing that irks me is when people say female and male instead of—or, I mean they use it as a noun instead of as an adjective. Like if you're saying "I can't stand when males do this or females do this," like that's just awkward. Like, are you not familiar with English? I'm pretty sure you're not supposed to do that [laughs]. It sounds gross to me, and I usually hear it with negative connotations especially. Like, you know. And that's one thing that irks me to heck, I can't stand it. Well, especially like the stuff boys write on Facebook. Like, "all females don't know blah blah blah" and I'm just like, shut the fuck up.

It is noteworthy that Awesome Woman includes multiple voices as she addresses the sociopolitical injustices she observes and experiences. Our conversation around her participation in Feminist Bootcamp revolved around an inclusion of subordinate voices:

> EB: You showed up to Feminist Bootcamp. I've had that link open on my computer since when you were over last—
> AW: There's a video of me on that.
> EB: Really? I totally want to see it [searching for video]. But, in my mind, I don't think that feminists are militant, you know. None of those stereotypical things. Even still, I'm like, I wonder what happened when she got there?... What does Feminist Bootcamp actually look like? Is everybody in camo or, do you know what I mean? And of course I know that they're not. But what does it look like?
> AW: It's definitely not—I definitely expected the organizers to be, I didn't know these organizers and they presented themselves as rich, white feminists. But I didn't know them—they wrote the Feminist Manifesto. But everybody who knew them loved them overall.
> EB: That's interesting because I was just reading about how so many people who do feminist art or feminist work often homogenize everything into a white middle-class experience. What's their book?
> AW: I forgot what it's called. *Young Feminist's Guide* to—it's like one of the first books in the Feminist Manifesto it's called…They're really nice women and I—it actually was more diverse than I expected, so I was okay with

	that. Although they are—or seems like they have this one book and they like—it could've been a homogenized experience, but it really wasn't. I thought I would be the only person of color, but there were like at least two other people of color, so there were three!
EB:	Out of a crowd of, like, fifty?
AW:	No, it wasn't that big. There were like twenty of us? It wasn't bad.
EB:	Where was it held?
AW:	At one of the theaters…Yeah, we had two older women too, which was kind of rare.
EB:	Cool…So, was it—did you feel like, did they do teach-ins on different ideologies and approaches to feminism?
AW:	No, it wasn't about that.… Every day was a focus. One day was the body. One day was reproductive justice. Everything was a new topic, and I think my favorite was the last one when it was the bodies. It was like body and images and, so first we talked to—we went to Columbia and we talked to this woman. She's a feminist and she's disabled. She's a professor. We talked to her and she was so beautiful. And, yeah she talked about a very important thing, about how when you talk about feminism it's supposed to include all. But you go to events and they're not wheelchair accessible. What does that say? … Yeah, I totally want to do the training and if after college, if I don't end up doing something else, I might try to be a full-time doula. Or so, yeah the woman who came when we were talking about ableism at Barnard. And I was thinking about how beautiful she is. And, so at my school we have something called "The Ism Project." So there is, it is through a center for multiculturalism. And they deconstruct "-isms," you know. They deconstruct ableism, but I want to do like a photoshoot with different disabled women. I think I want to have a gallery and not really talk about it, just show it. So she really just inspired me. People don't really focus. They only victimize, which is not fair.

In approaching topics of activism and action, it's interesting to consider what Awesome Woman conceives of as most imperative. She highlights the central role of educating, information sharing, and discussion in understanding others and connecting across differences as actions that lead to the creation of safer spaces for learning, care, and healing amongst communities.

· 9 ·

IMAGINING TACTICALLY STRATEGIC FUTURES

This chapter discusses implications from this study for future research designs. I briefly address nine levels of audience for this work, organized from micro to macro. I start with the reader, writer, and participants, and move to speak directly to audiences in the worlds of literacy and educational research. I then turn to speak to youth organizers, adult community activists, nonprofit managers, and policy makers invested in the sustainability and scalability of this work. All audiences are vital to continued justice-oriented activism.

Participants, Writer, Reader

To address ongoing considerations of and concerns for ethics, politics, and methodological rigor, I start with implications directly related to the participants. Gentle Meadows, Awesome Woman, Green Strawberries, Vaga De Franx, and People's Republic of Mars made this study possible. I maintain that our initial designs for research were ripe with transformative potential. While it was beyond the scope of this study to deeply engage with certain postfoundational hybridized research methods, the central importance of participant voice, input, and experience remains intact. The divergent histories, stories, and insights of the participants reflect a deep commitment to continued collaborative activist work around human rights and social justice with youth.

All of the participants were suggested to me as committed, vivacious, and visionary youth activists. They all entered the study with histories of activism, and each anticipated future uses of this study in their own work. As they move into full participation as adult actors in nonprofit management, human rights organizing, youth development, educational leadership, and international affairs contexts, it is my hope that this limited study sparks other research that extends our inquiry further. Stepping back, it will be interesting to further trace the trajectories of where their reflections, their visions, and their futures take them. Perhaps a follow-up collaborative study is in order.

As an educator deeply committed to studying adolescent literacy, the space of urban youth activism provided illustrative insights into elements of critical learning outside of school. As a poststructural cultural theorist, I am epistemologically located outside of more mainstream approaches to educational research. Thus, as the sole author of this text (despite the structured design for triangulation with and input from the participants), I recognize the ways in which I forced my fragmented, descriptive interpretation upon the reader. Even as I sought to take anti-authoritarian positions, it is true that writing remains a personal activity and each researcher carries an "I" from which they write, whether they choose to acknowledge it or not. This text thus necessarily serves as an articulation of myself as an activist educator researcher, and an articulation of the youth participants in specific moments of activism and organizing in their lives. Like other modes of documentation, writing makes a mark that locates the reader, the writer, and the participants in reconstructing specific junctures in time and history. This temporality should be celebrated. Future study calls for deeper inquiry around ethics in relation to participatory research and auto/ethnographic approaches to critical education growing out of the specific community-based needs of young people and their families to ensure that documentation is neither violent nor exploitative.

Researchers, Academics, Educators

Fundamentally, this work is about literacy. Although this study rhizomatically intersects with many connected topics, the impetus behind this research is to begin to better understand the ways in which youth activists engage in critical literacy as they undertake social action. This research could be reframed in many other lights, reflecting a heightened interest in and commitment to understanding social movement theory, urbanism, youth development, civic engagement, academic achievement, and more. Yet the function of this study remains explicitly and intricately tied to literacy and the attempt to identify opportunities for and examples of critical literacy learning operating without the limitations of school-based vertical organization and top-down dictum (Beck, 2005).

For literacy researchers, there is much to learn in the study of informal learning spaces outside school. Doing so outmaneuvers the school-based limitations to conducting critical literacy projects around such radical and contentious ideas as citizenship and democracy (Janks, 2013). This is not to say that educators and youth should be fearful of schools such that they don't seek to challenge the status quo around accountability and high-stakes testing. It is, however, to recognize that there is much we can accomplish by focusing on spaces of less formal education, such as contexts of organizing (Ginwright, 2010a). While there is no extant correlation (nor is one a necessity to validate such study), researchers from Morrell (2004) to Mira (2013) have provided evidence to suggest that youth who engage in organizing are more resilient, and their critical perspectives assist them in experiencing academic successes and matriculation to higher education. This study begins to address that gap, but more research is needed to develop a clearer picture of these connections.

Critical literacy, as a theory of literacy education and social change, serves in part to debunk stereotypes (Phelps, 2010). Such literacy does not exist in a vacuum, and praxis requires no specific context, save perhaps the stipulation of situated work. Throughout the study, participants revealed their political intentions (Lankshear & McLaren, 1993) through language that advances social critique and cultural transformations toward active refusal to reproduce oppressive ideologies (Knoblauch & Brannon, 1993). In fields ranging from New Literacy Studies (Street, 2003) to Blended Learning (Keengwe & Kang, 2013) and the Maker Movement (Santo, 2013), there is emergent evidence of new contexts for learning that simultaneously accentuates individual multimodal strengths and collectivizes community priorities. Various other public and academic spheres intersect with this work, highlighting the value of dialogue in examining perspectives on social and political topics (Comber, 2001). Social discourses bear the trace of other discourses from which they position their conceptual histories and trajectories. As such, educational researchers, political scientists, urban sociologists, and cultural theorists can leverage their skills and institutional resources to expand the discourse around innovative organizing spaces for critical literacy in activist action.

Cushioned within the wider world of scholarly writing for academic audiences, there is much to consider in further approaches to humanizing such social scientific study. Pushing the boundaries of peace and human rights research, of new social movement theories and urban development, of social justice and critical pedagogy, this study resituates youth activists as community knowledge builders in their learning, living, and work environments. There are innumerable anthropological, sociological, and psychological questions to explore around participatory action research and identity, focused specifically on literacy as well as wider schemas for studying youth in contemporary sociopolitical contexts. Moreover, there are deep epistemological questions to answer in the space between social justice-oriented work and postfoundational conceptions, interrogating methods to organize without essentializing. In doing so, such work matches the critical literacy call of Janks (2000), to consider how language creates social identities and how activist approaches can attend to diversity, plurality, and design.

This research is informative for educators working across the fields of curriculum, instruction, and learning. From early childhood to higher and continuing education, across urban, suburban, and rural contexts, there is strength in conducting situated work with youth around ideas of power, intelligence, and leadership in ways that support individual development and community initiatives. For pedagogical practices to be successful, they must respond to the sociohistorical contexts of the youth. Frequently, this is the domain of citizenship education but could extend deeply into youth participatory action research.

Cushioning critical literacy and youth organizing research in a discourse of civic engagement has the potential to offer a great breadth of transformative and/or indoctrinating results. Fundamentally, the distinction is answered through the question: what's your collectivist vision? Short-term answers for youth organizers might relate to specific issues they organize around in search of viable victories. More long-term conclusions are based on thinking about community development in ways that challenge exploitation, through studies of power and discrimination that take a design perspective to replicate critical literacy structures, to study rights education and build ethically activist curricula in ways that are intentionally and reflexively anti-oppressive.

Organizers, Organizations, Networks

Many community-based youth organizing projects take Freirean thematic investigation as a model for the creation of social justice-oriented youth development programs (Delgado & Staples, 2008). As an informal space of learning akin to models of popular political education, such projects support the design, development, and execution of conscientizing cultural actions in the context of local and larger geopolitical events (Shah, 2011). Such spaces of learning include workshops, outreach, campaigns, reflection, planning, commitment, resilience, and enduring visions of local/global communities. What would it mean to design, enact, and replicate such participatory pedagogy outside traditional classrooms? Partially, this involves creating texts, building tools, and initiating action around the nodes that define youth activist work. Such participation, when undertaken with overt social and political purpose, points to an answer to the question of what it means to be engaged critical citizens versus merely members of a mass audience.

Youth organizers use language and other symbolic systems (art, graffiti, music, performance) to interrogate discourses, language, and messages of bigotry and oppression (Ardizonne, 2007). The participants of the DKPNYC, with a shared background in human rights and social justice organizing, call for care and understanding as they mobilize themselves and each other against discriminatory and dehumanizing topics. They possess an inclination toward greater justice and equality with overt intentions toward learning about others. Speaking to all youth, this research advises: Be loud in your struggle for human rights and social justice. Silence to violence is itself a form of structural violence. Share your passions widely. There is great power in your truth.

There is a subtlety to this type of youth development work, which requires nuanced training and the investment of adult allies. Vaga De Franx, Gentle Meadows, and Awesome Woman all spoke at length about workshops, about creating opportunities for social and political learning in safe spaces. This reflects the need for a youth organizing pipeline to be established in community-based organizations, such that youth program participants can contribute to community organizing work as they become adults—thus perpetuating productive cycles of apprenticeship, mentoring, peer education, and critical teaching. For research on such a leadership pipeline, see Ginwright (2010b).

Further research is needed that includes community organizations to extend this line of inquiry into critical literacy in sociopolitical learning spaces outside school. Organizations like Global Kids, Fierce NYC, Brotherhood/SisterSol and many others are already doing this work, continually supporting youth to share their passionate, informed indignation around shared topics of identity and social injustice. Fundamentally, these organizing programs intersect around vital 21st-century competencies: developing literacy skills, participating in civic engagement, and constructing sociopolitical identities as leaders. There is a need to establish networks, to connect youth across towns and villages, regions, territories, states, nations, and other borders and divides. Despite the challenges of competing for limited foundation funding, there is potential for great connectivity by connecting young people, sharing resources, engaging multimodality, and creating opportunities to engage in forms of intellectual, social, and physical bordercrossing.

Lines of Flight: Trajectories of Space, Funding, and Futurity

As was highlighted by each participant, physical proximity is still important in organizing initiatives, but it is fundamentally different in a digital age. These youth activists demonstrated the ability to do the work of organizing and activism anywhere and everywhere. They push the boundaries of the local to consider online communities, cyber-actions, social networking, and more. All of the participants talked about information activism and connectivity. Collectively, the participants named the need for shared learning spaces in order to have time and space to discover sameness and to strategize around social justice, strength, resilience, and healing.

For its part, Global Kids and the Human Rights Activist Project—as well as workshops and programs at other organizations that the participants referenced—provided the space for these young people to identify relevant sociopolitical issues in their lives and engage a pedagogy of critical literacy to organize campaigns. This work was not done in a vacuum of radical activism. Rather, it was cushioned in the sphere of childhood and positive youth development. Continuing this work requires a level of sustained investment to create and maintain community spaces for learning, to fund after-school and out-of-school initiatives around literacy, justice, equity, and diversity. More observational organizational study is necessary to understand approaches to dynamic anti-oppressive learning through situated critical literacy and popular political education.

Extending a Research Agenda around Youth Organizing and Critical Literacy

Cushioned in the realm of recent research and writing on literacy and activism, conclusions around community and connectivity are multiple. The participant youth have pointed to the immediate and intersubjective nature of mobilizing themselves around a framework of human rights and social justice. They highlighted ways in which they learned to create a safe space for the interrogation of contrasting perspectives around a wide array of sociopolitical issues. They pointed to the value of exploring topics and interrogating mainstream U.S. media without falling into traps of moralism, hubris, or righteousness. While critiques abound around "nonpolitical" positiontaking and activism guided by ideas of "right," it is evident that youth organizing projects provide a space for the ethical expansion of forms of activist learning by engaging in variants of critical praxis (Ginwright & Cammarota, 2007). This idea of ethical activism requires deep consideration and exploration, to a greater extent than this study can afford.

Conclusions based on connectivity are important here to forward a conversation about building ethical networks for further refinement of critical literacy in out-of-school learning spaces. I can identify a host of ethical dilemmas in naming conclusions that proffer generalizations around youth organizing and activism. Thus Lather's (2007) concept of "transgressive validity" proves useful early and often in this work. Any and all answers to emerge out of this study come through forms of iterative meaning making, where individuals construct their activist identities in relation to the social and political. This study is personal and reported autobiographically, through lived histories and memories of organizing work. To understand such constructions with any depth, it is important to focus the gaze on the youth themselves, on their activist pursuits around consumption, production, and dissemination of information through multiple routes.

Following Mouffe (1993), definitions around activism are not about establishing a baseline against which to determine who qualifies as an activist but rather about how activist identities are constructed and articulated in social and historical contexts. In light of this knowing, the idea of positiontaking proves important in alluding to an iterative subjectivity, in which individuals choose to act and articulate the self through each moment and event of activism. In practice, the youth involved in this study defined their activist identities as they questioned the prioritization of issues. At the same time, they look at interconnected, multiple topics for informed activism, identifying contradiction in consideration of future actions. Thus are they always and repeatedly becoming activist.

Future study of youth organizing should seek to examine the construction and development of sociopolitical identities in relation to the motivation of individuals and groups to engage, mobilize, and join actions around specific and diverse justice-oriented issues. Despite the limitations of resources and funding to approach vast and sometimes disparate topics, the participants of this study demonstrated great willingness toward collectivity. Their conclusions pointed to the benefits of further study around overtly political, positive youth development programming in community-based organizations to create and support a safe space that is not always accentuated in other contexts of campaigning and organizing. There is a necessity for such spaces of education across multiple contexts and borders, of the global North and global South, across economic, cultural, and sociopolitical divides, both in person and online.

I pause to acknowledge my researcher voice here, as I have attempted to do throughout. The conclusions I have drawn in writing are limited based on my operation as a writer, a thinker, and a social justice-oriented critical educator. In my practice, I demonstrate similar levels of outrage against injustice and inequity as the participants articulate themselves. Despite our differences, we are very similar as we speak up against discriminatory bigotry. It makes people uncomfortable when the status quo is shaken and dominant violence is challenged, but it is a huge part of activist work in defense of human rights, which itself is a value-laden framework for situated organizing projects.

It is important to note that this study was not built solely around a privileging of human rights activism as the only approach to conducting social justice-based work. Still, there are shared concepts and modes of communication that are highlighted by the participants by nature of their involvement with HRAP. Thus, there is similarity in these youth activists, even as they question the essentialization of their unique identities. Despite differences on issues, the participants shared platforms of human rights and approaches to peer education and community-based learning that are intentionally anti-oppressive. Even though personal connections to the issues initially motivated these individuals toward activism and organizing, all the participants named intersubjective extensions outside their immediate social worlds. They spoke of this much as I talk about ethics that don't moralize through a queer theory of activism: in acknowledgment of sameness and deferral of definition in the struggle for creating complex identities built around dignity, respect, safety, freedom, and health. Doing so is to acknowledge the inherently political while refusing to submit to the traps of the poststructural cliché.

As a knowledge worker, I introduce a queer theory of activism as one conclusion that spawns research futurity. Ginwright's (2010a) idea of "radical healing" is crucial here—not just for urban youth but also for all marginalized (young) people. Exploring the history of social movements and expanding the self-reporting of youth from such movements adds substantially to the understanding of the motivation for and the approaches to activist learning and organizing. Here enters the ethical in the realm of the nonhierarchical and nonmoralistic. The interconnection of issues around anti-oppressive tenets posits a queer theory of activism that expands the conversation of difference beyond the sole documentation and tolerance of or acceptance for pluralistic diversity.

Considering and reconsidering the idea of organizing around identity politics and single-issue topics is at once fruitful and requires troubling. Following Pinar (1998) and Kumashiro (2002), a queer theory of activism takes an ethical approach to working around dominant and normalizing discourses. It creates a condition for an approach to social justice and human rights activism that does not moralize on the grounds of right—except, perhaps, in the pursuit of peaceableness, equity, and freedom. This is not to downplay the politicized stances of the participants and myself nor to assume legitimacy of those ideological terms and concepts. Of course, these terms and positions are political and have traces of morality written upon them, ceaselessly signifying through their connotative connections toward motivation, desire, perception, interpretation, and action. Despite the constancy of erasure and redefinition, there is power in decentering deferral.

Forms of activist queering around issues of identity related to minoritized or nonnormative positiontaking extend discussions of language, power, and social justice through nondominant discursive disruption. Through choices about the words and ways in which we speak of our identities, we make choices to include political labels in our lives and/or to defer/submit to categorization. The loose definition of community that comes out of such a queered theory is not always placebased, but it is nonsectarian as it looks across multiple perspectives on issues. Highlighting the importance of safe space in one's own life is key to connecting across identity groups locally, nationally, and globally. A queer theory of activism provides a framework in which youth organizers gather around issues that foreground a politics of difference in an effort to provide just and equitable spaces for growth and learning, creating opportunities for subordinate groups of individuals to participate and engage in activist spaces, in person and online.

This work is rooted in postfoundational ideas of/in/against deconstruction and poststructuralism. As a researcher and a writer, my work has for many years been acutely focused on exploring particular, political sites of intensity without providing normative options. Inquiry ad infinitum. By not judging the function of power/knowledge in overtly moralistic terms, such a postfoundational position rather serves to expose negotiable spaces of resistance. I remain committed to the continued interrogation of oppressive power/knowledge functions. I aim to further explore uses of queer theory as an underexplored vantage from which to explore the multiple ways that power functions in relation to identity, ways that are neither unified nor singular in their approach. This is as true of the term "activist" as it is of any other articulation of a constructed identifier.

My approach to the data in this study involved reading, reporting, and retelling in ways that were exemplar without being representative. In part, this is related to varied interactions with (con)texts and articulations of activist selves in light of such interaction. Such texts not only shed light on how participants articulate themselves as activists, but they are also key elements to illustrate how and why youth become activists, what that means to them, or why anyone should pay attention. The participants' self-articulated visions of themselves in relation to these rights- and justice-oriented identities speak to the need to understand social activist organizing on multiple levels of learning theory and practice.

Building networks around literacy learning and youth organizing offers the space to share cultural and educative resources for critical pedagogy and restorative social justice practices. Lots of authors write about critical pedagogy, just as many people wax on the definitions of literacy. Mayo Jr.'s (2013) article about critical pedagogy and gay-straight alliances in *Educational Researcher* reflects the timeliness and relevance of thinking, writing, talking, and organizing around activist queering. Such activist projects offer a space for both individual and collective identities to be defined through a refinement of the tools of reflexive social and political action, with skills and processes emerging where positive youth development meets community-based organizing. Understanding the functional operations of these tools is the challenge for literacy researchers, critical pedagogues, and community organizers alike to develop schema and spaces for certain forms of replication, application, and scalability of humanizing organizing pedagogies.

Of course, markers and measures of effective social justice action, organizing, and activism are wide reaching, from building a critical mass and growing a base to boycotting industries, lobbying policy, stopping traffic, and various other interpretations of interrupting the status quo. I initially drafted these conclusions as the U.S. Justice Department was actively seeking the extradition of Edward Snowden from Russia and Pfc. Bradley Manning was up for 136 years in prison for his role as a whistleblower—or as leaker/traitor/hero, depending on one's perspective. These individuals and others demonstrate with great severity that information is important, dangerous, and powerful; that language matters a great deal in rights-based activism and learning. Multidisciplinary foci on new media studies, critical media literacy, and multimodal competencies are essential in the current social and political economy. There is a need to build, fund, and support organizational intentionality around youth organizing (O'Donoghue, 2006). The next level of networked and resourceful organizing and community activism with youth requires spaces that celebrate literacy, voice, history, curiosity, diversity, and language.

So what is the prescription? Nonprescriptive activist thinking: building communities and identities around care and healing while moving away from all forms of violence (psychological, institutional, physical, emotional, psychic, structural, and otherwise). Of course we cannot reject our dominant contexts, but we can focus on expanding interpretations to yield a larger knowledge base. As Pinar (1998) wrote in his seminal text on queer theory in education, "The crucial battle now for 'minorities' and resistant subalterns is not achieving democratic representation but wrestling control over the discourses concerning identity construction" (p. 7). Our work is thus the struggle to counterattack those supremacists that actively silence, oppress, marginalize, and displace.

This requires space to counternarrate. I call it counterspace. As the youth participants in this study noted, the future of online organizing lacks a physical space for interpersonal presence. The creation and maintenance of a counterspace would fill the need for a community-based physical locale from which to self-organize, designing arenas to encourage critical literacy learning and allow a diversity of individuals to organize together. This physicality can take many forms: DIY maker media collectives, organizing workshops, popular education seminars, art shows, teach-ins, conferences, celebrations, and other safe spaces for cross-cultural, intersubjective exchange.

"Becoming activist" is more about fluid movement than it is about evolution. This study forwards a conception of complex human identity (de)construction as constitutive even while development occurs. The shared work for critical literacy and youth organizing is to create a capacity for physical, psychological, intellectual, and emotional border crossing (Giroux, 2005), for understanding across radical difference (Welch, 1991). This requires working together beyond the boundaries of identity, beyond nationality, against compartmentalization, hubris, ignorance, hatred, and negativity. It calls instead for us to build community consciousness, raise the level of discourse, cultivate resilience, and envision ways to reinvent ourselves beyond oppressive conditions.

The challenge for organizing collectively and connecting youth activists is in cultivating these disparate community nodes. Facing that challenge, there exists a palpable opportunity to establish youth organizing as a powerful model of youth leadership around ethics, politics, education, and citizenship (Heinz, 2012). This is as true locally as it is nationally and globally. As I conclude writing this section, Egypt is in a state of violent turmoil and the death toll in Syria is rising. The call to antiviolence is only getting ever louder. The scope of this work is both macro and micro in negotiating futures of human rights activism and supporting significant roles for youth in such struggle, in their most local contexts and in their most global visions.

Such negotiations require a focus on language, understood broadly in terms of sign systems and the power functions around signification. This reifies the centrality of literacy research in learning about and refining pedagogical models based on organizing. Discursively, the work of social justice and human rights organizing draws many parallels to the elements of critical literacy, replicating issue-based praxis as codified through a literacy-driven taxonomy. There is much left unexplored in the connection between the rich fields of youth organizing and critical literacy, both at once located as vital subgenres of the academy and as intentionally defiant outliers.

I could write much more with the study participants. We barely scratched the surface of their impassioned activism documented here. Vaga De Franx, Gentle Meadows, Green Strawberries, People's Republic of Mars, and Awesome Woman all talked in multiple directions with divergent trajectories, detailing specific issues with specific tactics ranging from legal advocacy to civil disobedience and radical revisioning of social intersectional interactions. In doing so, these youth activists and their wider social worlds of educators, researchers, and community organizers demonstrated the capacity to contribute to a network of ethical learners who move beyond moralizing, beyond tolerance, to add their trajectories to combat oppression and create new options for learning. There is much yet to understand about the practices of literacy learning in spaces of youth organizing. Future research must consider the role of the word, the environment, and the activist in the social justice struggles of a digital, globalized future.

· 1 0 ·

STEP FIVE: REFLECTING AND ENVISIONING ACTIVISMS

The fifth and final element in the critical literacy taxonomy involves reflecting upon actions taken and creating vision(s) for future project(s). While all of the participants approached activism and organizing in unique ways, they shared the context of an investment in the protection and defense of human rights. Whether they physically rallied students and workers or digitally created art and organized information for dissemination online, all of the participants engaged in social justice actions and forms of human rights activism. Further, all of the youth participants talked about their future activist work by first reflecting on the past. This is striking as a clear example of praxis (Freire, 1970; Lankshear & McLaren, 1993), reflecting on action taken to envision the next steps towards social change.

Vaga De Franx: Reflection for Futurity

As we turned to talk about the future, Vaga De Franx reflected on her past and the lessons she learned as an organizer and an activist with Occupy Wall Street:

> VDF: I think that, you know, we knew that when the winter hit, it was going to be hard. You're talking about an outside encampment, you're talking

people's health, about being responsible for that, so obviously it thinned out and people dissipated a little bit, but I still see people in the subway who are wearing Occupy Wall Street T-shirts and you just know. And when you asked me before, what is better, the local organizing or these big encounters? I think that the big encounters and the general assemblies, it builds momentum.

She noted the continued restlessness despite the lack of a location for the movement, pointing to the need for a space where organizing for economic and social justice can continue. Her current work with information activism involves and includes the creation and dissemination of a magazine dedicated to free university access:

VDF: And so when we are creating the 'zine, which is a student-led publication, it's the ideas of the students, right? But it's also, what sources are we using? Because we are not going to use textbooks, we are not going to use the *New York Times*; I'm not going to use those resources. We're going to use the books that we are reading, you know, how they affected how we look at the world, but also using these books to bring about our own conclusions, and our own ideas, and our own theories, you know? Essentially, we are going to be the next authors, and the next professors, and the next teachers. So, you know, just like they're changing the way we are thinking about things now, we are going to change the way that people are going to think about things later on. So, we have to get our information from good sources, but realize that they are just sources. We need to come up with our own analysis of the society that we live in. And we have been, and when I start talking to students about an issue, and they start talking to me, you know, they end up coming up with things that they didn't know they had in them. As they are talking, they realize these things and the next thing you know they come to a big conclusion that maybe you didn't know! And the book that they were reading allowed them to get there. So the 'zine is going to be kind of like that. Because there are so many things we want to say. So it's going to be an analysis like that, and we are going to come up with that ourselves. And there is no place in the classroom to really express that to each other. You know, one of the things I keep saying is that we keep having these meetings and we never get anything done because we keep talking about the stuff we are reading, and our society, and our analysis on it. And the next thing you know, our meeting has stopped and we are not doing anything so you know, it's like, how can we get this information outside of this meeting room where there is only ten people, out to people who really need to know. And it's things that you can't say in the classroom; it's too radical, things like that. You know, we can't hold events every week and expect everyone to come. But if we can put it in a

STEP FIVE: REFLECTING AND ENVISIONING ACTIVISMS   111

        'zine, then that is something that you can carry in your pocket and share with people. And someone asks where can you find that, and you say they left a stack in the library, and all of the sudden people start exchanging information. And it's there, you know, whenever you want it. And it's written by your fellow classmates so you don't feel like you're being taught from the top down.

EB: It's interesting, too, because you're talking about something that is physical and concrete, and so much of the information that we are talking about now is digital and in a new way so—it just seems like a really striking juxtaposition to make something tangible. It's becoming more interesting to me all the time asking about who is controlling this information, and who can shut down any information at any time. And it's not tangible because people put so much trust in Google Docs and the cloud. And the information can be gone depending on how radical the concepts that you're coming with are.

VDF: Yeah. The more I organize, the more wary I become of all these websites and the more I realize I have so many emails at my IP address. Is that bad? But yeah, definitely having something that can't be stopped because it is physical at the end of the day. And you can't stop people from talking about it. You can't stop people from passing each other this. Even if we can't distribute inside the library, we can keep it in our book bags and distribute it on campus and things like that.

This reflection on the divide between physical and digital information came up multiple times over the course of the study. It relates in many ways to ideas of information sharing and connectivity, as we attempt to locate safe spaces for learning that cannot be censored or silenced.

We continued to reflect on issues of local autonomy and network building as she discussed her current and future work. She highlighted the need for organizational intentionality and collaborative dynamics with fellow organizers and activists as they planned actions. As we concluded, I asked her for her vision and plans for future action:

EB: So maybe talk just a little about some of the larger global implications you see. Because you were talking about Quebec and Mexico and Chile and I was talking about Spain. What kind of networks do you envision? Because when I do this work and talk to you and some of the other participants, I wonder what we will connect into or build out of? And what kind of larger international student movements do we see?

VDF: Like the New World Order alternative? [laughs]

EB: [laughing] Yeah, an anti-oppression option. But what do you envision? Do you think that the work—because I know you believe in local work and

VDF: always working in your neighborhood and on community. But, going to scale—do you see that happening?

VDF: See, that's the thing. I think that locality is what would actually make a larger-scale movement work because—and I do think about that a lot. Students have to nationally link up with the working class, the workers, different sectors of the population. But you know, being in touch with student movements abroad, we have realized that it's important to build those ties on a larger scale and nationally have that movement strong. But none of it is going to work unless every neighborhood and every community starts implementing safe space. Starts implementing educational programs, social programs, starts offering resources and spreading resources. It's not, you're not going to be able to form those ties if you don't have a strong—you can't just have three people, three student leaders from Chile talking to three student leaders from the United States. Doesn't mean that those connections can't happen, but it has to include a lot more people. It has to include localities and—I guess the reason I do emphasize locality is because I want to see the larger-scale connection and that larger-scale movement. And I know that the only reason that is going to happen is if localities are strong and communities are strong. You can't—if you have these movements in which three students here and three students there are communicating, then you just kill those off and you are done. Nobody else knows about it and nobody else—there's not a community back there that is going to mobilize itself. So I emphasize locality because I want to see that. But you have to get it from the root and then work your way up…and then you see schools in other parts of the city wanting to organize and start their own thing. And so we have kept those connections.

Before we concluded, she told me about efforts to connect youth organizers across the country, particularly focusing on building networks with young people in "middle America." The event, called the National Student Power Convergence, was to take place near the end of the summer of 2012:

VDF: It's a national convergence that people are literally donating two dollars to because this isn't covered by some big grant. This is something that we need, and it's something that we are organizing and we are building donation funds and fundraisers here and there. Whatever it takes to make it happen. But it's going to be the first national student empowerment convergence that grassroots groups have organized. And, you know, we are hoping to build that connection and start that student unity—a student union for example. And we've learned a lot even this year. Folks that last year, at our retreat, were like no student union, no centralization, no this and this and that. They see what is going on in Quebec and Chile and this year around, at the student conference, student union is one of the biggest topics. So, you know, it all happens on its own. Sometimes, I get caught up in trying to envision the future and trying to envision all of this. But when I sit back and think where I was a year ago and where our organization was a year ago, it's all happening. All you can do is strengthen your own community and your own campus so that when that time comes, we are a good student group who are able to participate…So learning that—just patience—has been really helpful.

Gentle Meadows: A Vision on the Future through the Past

When Gentle Meadows talked about his future, he reflected on family and history:

GM: It's kind of funny, like how your study asks how literacy is involved. Like, when I—when I look at my grandparents, I don't know if I'd say that they were activists, but a certain part of me wants to say it. Like, there are definitely issues that they are passionate about. But, and on other issues, I wouldn't say they were very progressive about it. Like, for example, they think that America is a very cruel place and people are too individualistic around here. And like, when they watch the news and see how the Bush tax cuts, how there are talks about them being extended, they are just like—why would he do that? Even coming from a background in Southeast Asia, which is not the most liberal society or form of government. Like, wealth distribution is a good thing. Like, maybe it's not happening, but the average person thinks that it is generally a good thing. But here in America, they think that it is always being questioned. And that there is this thinking in America that someone is poor and it is their fault. But they don't think that. So, sometimes they look at it from a very Christian point of view, like that we should feed the poor, feed the hungry, take care of your neighbor. And I think that is advocacy, whether or not it has religious or Christian message… It's a form of—it's definitely a way to connect with other issues. So, becoming activist, I don't know how to say it. You can't pinpoint it, but…

As we concluded our discussion, he talked a little about a vision for his future activism, as well as identifying pressing needs for others engaging in social justice work:

GM: Well, what I see from my university, the racial diversity needs to be improved. So like, focus on literacy. How is that defined? Is it words

	written on a page? Or is it dialogue, incorporated in that term? In a way, I don't know, I hate myself for saying this but literacy sometimes, or writing things down, as opposed to the oral tradition, it's a very Eurocentric thing imposed on the rest of the world. So, from an anti-imperialist perspective, can literacy incorporate oral tradition or discuss things not on paper, but…
EB:	What do you think? Do you think it can?
GM:	I mean, I feel like people could have different answers. I mean, I like literacy. More people should be literate with reading and writing. And learn from that, and develop as a human being from words on paper. I mean, I like both. Like, you can't just choose one. I mean, oral tradition is good but it also has its limits. Same thing with writing.
EB:	Which is interesting, too, when you think about new media. Because it's like the fusion of so many things…
GM:	It's good that there are more—many different types of mediums out there to communicate ideas. Like, I forgot who said it, that the Medium is the Message.
EB:	Oh, Marshall McLuhan. Totally.
GM:	Yeah, that's who it is. Like, there should be more mediums out there.
EB:	Yeah, definitely, when I think about the future of doing this kind of work, researching and connecting with youth activists and organizing groups, a huge part of it is to see how they are creating a future. And how we all create messages for ourselves and others in different ways.
GM:	The "how" question is really important.

Green Strawberries: Radical Self-Reflection

Green Strawberries reflected on the past as she talks about her present. It is noticeable how strongly she critiques the Left in regards to issues of race, gender, and class.

EB:	You think that Occupy is successful at all?
GS:	I think that Occupy has been successful in branches, not as a whole.
EB:	Okay.
GS:	I feel like the immigration and the union perspective has definitely been successful. I don't really feel like many others are really doing anything. I have been hearing a lot about how a lot of people in Occupy Wall Street are not for focusing on undocumented immigration. That's just not an issue. Which makes me think, this is mostly by white people, right?

Through her continued critiques, she returns to (re)create a vision for the future. When I asked her about her vision, she went on a long aside about

STEP FIVE: REFLECTING AND ENVISIONING ACTIVISMS   115

attending a socialist conference in Chicago with Gentle Meadows, documenting the sexism she experienced there. Her plans and steps for the future are connected to this remembrance:

> EB: Where do you imagine it taking you in the future?
> GS: Honestly, I just see myself [laughs]. Here's the thing. I don't have one of those five-year plans…Even my degree, which I moved to political science recently. I have the degree, awesome, I'll do something with it. But really, I am going to focus on, I would really love to move to a Middle Eastern or South Asian country for a while, but live with the indigenous…But I feel like, the problem with that is, I'm being very individualistic in that way. Because I'm going away from a collective to find my own self as a person of color. So really, that's my only plan so far. And hopefully, if I really do that and it truly happens, I can come back with a better, more radicalized perspective and take it even further. I definitely see myself becoming more and more and more radical as time goes by. And I see that because of the people I am connected to also.

People's Republic of Mars: Envisioning Activism and Advocacy

This focus on Internet organizing informed our discussion of his reflection on the past and his goals for future activism. When I asked him about the future, he encouraged me to continue to connect with human rights organizers internationally. He noted that it is a difficult struggle to develop a network of organizers "that is not so much censored or edited by diplomatic channels."

When I asked him for his vision for the future, he returned to the intentions and objectives behind the Millennium Development Goals because they "pretty much cover everything." As an activist and an organizer, he had more specific plans for himself:

> PRM: Well, right now I'm trying to expand my organization. Get the 501(c)(3). So, I am looking for lawyers that could guide me through the 501(c)(3). It's a long process, so… I want to do more activism because it's a human rights organization. But, I am going to do the implementation of human rights, but at the same time do a lot of activism here in the U.S. and even in other countries when we expand. So that's my goal, you know. There have been organizations, Human Rights Watch and Amnesty International, but I want to do more ground work and more like, radical activism but you

know—not necessarily violent or anything. So, that's my goal. That's the plan. Let's just see how things go.

Before he left our interview to head to a day full of meetings at his university, I asked him one last question: why did he choose People's Republic of Mars as his pseudonym?

PRM: Well, like I said, it's just like a utopia. It's an ideal place for me. Because Mars has not been inhabited yet. So I just feel like, it could be a new beginning and a new world. And if you start a new world, you want to make sure that everything you messed up in this world gets—you get to start anew, in a way. You could start everything from a fresh beginning. Yeah, so that was the thinking process there, People's Republic of Mars. And also, it's a people's republic. It's not like a dictatorship or anything else. A people's republic. I always prefer giving people the voice.

Awesome Woman: Performing the Unwritten

One thing that is noteworthy in dialogue with Awesome Woman is the way in which she includes competing narratives and counternarratives in a larger conversation around identity. As a performer, both theatrically trained and conceptually focused, she ceaselessly pushes into new terrain. She invited me to a show before our final interview:

EB: Tell me about the *Hijabi Monologues*.
AW: Oh no, that performance was postponed. But this Saturday, we are doing a limited performance. It's free. It's for Global Deaf Muslim. So they are trying to put together sign language for the Qur'an. They want to have the Qur'an in sign. You should see some of the videos—it's so intense. The girls are saying things like "We're deaf, not dumb." And they are trying to come up with signs for certain phrases… But different words and the signing of them. It's really fascinating.
EB: Yeah, it is.
AW: So, what happened was our room got cancelled. So, I reserved space at the university. Because of some bullshit, it got cancelled. They had another event at the same time as our event. And they were like, "Hey, can you move your event?" And we were like, "No, we can't move our event." And the Law School had moved their event to another day. So they invited us. So, although it is a limited performance, we are getting an honorarium so that is cool. And they are going to have people sign what we are saying, which is incredibly cool. The *Hijabi Monologues* itself—that is a piece of activism.

EB: Yeah, that's what I am thinking. So, break it down.

AW: So, Sahar—her name is Sahar Ullah. She went to Stanford and it talked about her experience with some of her classmates. And one of her good friends, he is a white Christian man. And he was like, you should write everything you are saying and perform those words out. And she was like, ok, and she started writing. And she had a show at Stanford and then she went out—what she says is, I feel like I'm quoting her now, is that her show was inspired by the *Vagina Monologues*, in which she takes something private and makes it public. And Sahar, her vision is to take something that everyone is talking about, and make it more private. Because women are telling different stories. And the hijab is not the center of the story—it's a prop. It's just a prop, yeah. But the story, they are talking with their perspectives on the Hijabi, or on being a Muslim. So you don't necessarily have to be Hijabi, that is the one who wears the hijab, to tell the story because it is still part of your life whether you wear it or not. So I like—I am fascinated with this project. And I'm part of the cast.

EB: So you are performing at universities and other places?

AW: Yeah, so we performed so far—we have only performed in one other—this is going to be our second performance. We performed at this graduate student residence hall, another limited performance, of students at Columbia and other students in the city. And so, I really love the project because it is not trying to be political, it is just telling a story. And I feel like that in itself is an act. Just to open your mouth and tell a story that everyone else is talking about. And to say, "I have a stake in this, here's my perspective." And they also do, at the end of every show, there is a question and answer, and there are feedback sheets because she is always trying to update the show and make sure that whatever message is out there, that it translates. So I can say that one piece that is part of the show is this woman who, she's walking, it's called "49th and 5th" and she's from Ohio originally, and she is visiting New York during the time of the Park 51 Center, that whole issue, and she's coming and she's really fearful. And she is walking in Times Square and she's really fearful, and that was just a couple of months after the Times Square bombings.

EB: Right.

AW: So, she is walking in this area and she is just like highly aware and really scared. Things are going on around her. She is being followed by this woman, and she doesn't know why, and she feels like she is going to be attacked. And the woman's like, "Can I hug you?" And the woman is like, "You want to hug me? You stopped me in this crazy busy place to hug me?" And she said, "Well, I come from a place of hate." She was from Israel, and she was like "This hug, seeing you is like, it civilizes a future for hope." And so, people were touched by it, but the story and what it is about—it's just like, wow. I'm a walking representation always. So that is what it was like for me. Because at first, I didn't even pick up on that second part. I

	was like, this is really cute. But then—that's me. You know? And I'm just like—damn, she is a representation. That is the whole idea of this. And I find a lot of people don't get that. Or you have to—or they don't care. And I'm really excited about that story, and it was done very well.
EB:	That's very interesting, especially because a lot of what this project is about is about how you perform your activist self every day.

Awesome Woman engages in deep reflection and visioning around her activism, from early design and institutional programming to direct action and public performance. As a trained performer, she pushes past borders of gender and sexuality, tapping a shared social justice discourse space that is not known in many cultural circles:

EB:	We have already talked about performance, and it sounds like you have got a lot of stuff going on there. So I wrote, where do you see your involvement in activism going in the future? Do you have any ideas?
AW:	I'm really interested in sexual harassment. Like, sexual harassment in my community and in communities at large. Like I feel like it's ridiculous that we have to walk around and be harassed, that that is just normalized. Like even the way we teach it to kids. Like, we can tell the boys "This is how you talk to a girl," but we tell the girls, "Don't talk to boys." It's really messed up. Like, how do you—we can't do that, basically. You can't tell girls like, "don't get raped." And then you say to guys, "Have as many girls as you want. You're free, the world is yours." And it's just like, why can't you say the same thing to the girl? Why can't it be? Why is she called a slut or a whore when she's having a healthy sexual relationship? She can do whatever. Why can't she do that if he can do that? And so, it's just sending weird messages to our kids. And clearly it's being played out when we see TV and like, why? So, like, for example, when we talked about, oh, someone was calling Kim Kardashian a whore because she slept with all of these guys. And I'm like, well, she is dating Kanye West. Do you think that he's a whore? Because he's probably a whore too—like he's definitely a whore, it's not even a question [laughing]. So why are we doing this? And I feel like, I'm really not about—I don't want to raise my kids in a woman-hating society. And so I am, I really want to promote equality in all ways. So sexual harassment, and sex education, I want to talk about all these things. I think it's important that everyone receives it. I don't mean just condoms. Like, total sexual health. I think it's really sad that women don't know they have a cervix, or what does it do.

In her visions for the future, Awesome Woman offers more than I could ever encapsulate on the page. I asked why she agreed to be a part of this study about activism and literacy:

AW: I agreed because one, it's you! And I'm really—I just want to help out in any way and I'm really interested in being documented and seeing what work will come out of this and will it be useful to me in the future. So that's my reason for being involved. I imagine we are going to meet all the other participants and exchange ideas. I don't really know what is going to come from it but I imagine some of the other people you are meeting with are also artists and they might be interested in the same kinds of things that I'm interested in. On that level, it can become a very social interaction. Also, I feel like we might be able to produce things and organize in the future. Also, I do expect a book. That is what I hope will happen. That's what I want to happen for you!

EB: There will be a book.

AW: Yay! And I definitely want it to be a text I will be able to use in the future for whatever reason. I don't imagine my life in the future as me just being a teacher and that's it. That's not me. I'm never just doing one thing. I'm always involved. And I do see activism continuing to be a part of my life until I die.

· 1 1 ·
ARTICULATING ACTIVIST IDENTITIES

Vaga De Franx

Vaga De Franx articulated her identity as an undocumented student and community organizer. She is committed to local organizing and involves herself with citywide coalitions of other self-identified social justice activists. She identified moments and situations of injustice, such as a lack of access to affordable higher education in New York City, to organize against economic stratification and exclusion. She located her activism in relation to her personal life and her learning. In doing so, she highlighted the importance of understanding our histories through international, independent sources and using the mainstream media against itself. She made deep inquiries into who produces information and policy positions around topics such as the War on Drugs and the NYPD's Stop and Frisk. She positioned her own activist work in relation to international struggles, building off of international models while recognizing the unique makeup of her communities in New York.

As an organizer, she facilitated anti-oppressive learning around publishers, Marxists, liberals, and progressives through peer education, study groups, teach-ins, and workshops. In that context, she asked probing questions that focus on elements such as shared readings, generative brainstorms, collective experiences, and the creation of a space for stories. She dissected the importance of and challenges around creating safe space for nonsectarian educative sessions. At the same time, she troubled elements of ideology in relationship to activism, advocating for forms of neutrality that do not push immovable political positions.

For Vaga De Franx, to be an activist means to be focused on the social and the political. She moved fluidly between discussions of planning major events that build momentum to sustaining local, autonomous activism that is not dictated by top-down organizing. In multiple ways, she articulated a frequent refrain that localities have to be strong in order for wider networks to sustain and grow. It is apparent that she defined her activism, in part, by the struggle for community access to resources, as much of her work is related to issues around immigration and education. In this pursuit, she called for continued patience, listening, and healing.

One lasting notion Vaga De Franx offered is that the skills of community-based social justice organizing and human rights activism can be reinvented in multiple locales in relation to many different issues. From Bloombergville to Occupy Wall Street and Occupy CUNY, her activist identity is not encapsulated in a single moment. It is a life pursuit to work against repression. She builds herself and her community with the tools to protect themselves from risk of censorship, arrest, and deportation, sharing information with stakeholders in communities that are being oppressed. From physical 'zines to Internet networking, she took a nuanced approach to information freedom and the dangers implicit in activist sharing. She positioned herself as an activist beyond institutional dogmatism, articulating an argument that no one should be silenced or intimidated for their actions. She ended our discussions for the study by talking about future plans for the National Student Convergence, acknowledging organizers as tools in sociopolitical community struggle, and laughing about building a New World Order alternative.

Gentle Meadows

Gentle Meadows quietly articulated his activist identity. In this study, he positioned himself first in relation to the moments of his youth in the immigrant neighborhoods in Queens where he grew up and attended school. Much of his activist roots are connected to his time in Global Kids and his involvement with the citywide coalition of the Human Rights Activist Project. He highlighted the importance of conversation and dialogue as foundational for learning and growing, gaining multiple perspectives and coming to understand the experiences of others.

In his articulation of himself as an activist and organizer, his humility downplayed his deep knowledge about issues around international affairs, state security, and human rights. As he remembered the work he did when he was in high school around food production, the wars in Iraq and Afghanistan, Israel and Palestine, women's rights and LGBTQ rights, he pointed to the importance of having safe spaces for learning. He argued that the elements of such workshops focused on positive youth development structures that make space for social justice organizing, to discuss controversial topics and work past barriers to create peaceable, actionable visions.

Gentle Meadows stressed the need to politicize issues. In his activist work, he continually studied topics of marginalization, human rights, nation-state rights, and the concept of welfare. He highlighted the interconnections between complex social issues and argued that human rights activists need to engage in a struggle even if it is not personally related to one's experience. He evoked Judith Butler to talk about the performance of identity and the performance of statehood. In doing so, he highlighted the notion that discourse spaces are ripe for catalyzing change for individuals and institutions. He argued that not taking hard political lines allows for things to become gray and for possibilities of change to be realized through rich dialogues and narratives.

His activist work ranged from his early interviews in New York's Union Square around same-sex marriage equality to his more recent work around socially just investiture and community literacy. As Gentle Meadows talked about the Socially Responsible Investing Committee at his school, he was clearly skeptical about the university and questioned the real power behind shareholder advocacy. He argued that activists challenge oppressive discourses around justice and access. As he stated early in our study, activists connect people through being socially aware and engaging with the communities in which they are involved. As such, he championed information freedom in his own view on contemporary issues in the digital present. He named Bradley Manning in this discussion, arguing that action is not always about physicality and that information should be transparent and free. He reinforced the notion that although human rights activists and social justice organizers often have different goals, it is the process that connects them.

Green Strawberries

Green Strawberries articulated her activist identity as she teased out the benefits and challenges at work in the constitution of Leftist political organizing. At the time of the study, she was involved in organizing political events for Occupy Wall Street. She identified herself as more of an organizer than an activist. In saying so, she made the distinction between activists who show up at events and organizers who make it possible for events to happen.

As an organizer, she was skeptical of the operations of online organizing, even as she recognized its benefits. When I spoke to her, I frequently thought of the Indignados in Spain. She embodied indignation when it came to standing up against dehumanization, both online and in physical spaces of organizing. She argued that there is a deep need for activists to connect to people already involved with struggles "on the ground." Green Strawberries challenged the fractured branches of Occupy Wall Street, critiquing the operations of the white labor movement's cooptation of Occupy's moment. She pointed out the difficulty of organizing without a unified message on the Left, a criticism leveled from many political perspectives.

Despite the divergence of topics, Green Strawberries had clear elements from cultural history, media, and current events through and against which she positioned herself. She accessed much of her information from blunt, international news. She focused her organizing around issues related to immigration and education, as she had many friends and associates who struggled to get access to civic resources and higher learning. She created activist artifacts around the struggle of the Palestinian people, speaking in depth about her street art around Palestine and her desire to live in the Middle East to live and feel connected to her heritage. In her radical activist pursuits, she argued that organizing and activism are more than spectacle. She pointed to the crucial work of community building and challenged the political Left in the U.S. to find similarities to organize around, even when the ideological lines force differences.

People's Republic of Mars

People's Republic of Mars articulated his activist identity in relation to his deep knowledge of public health, international affairs, and foreign policy. He is situated in a space where diplomacy intersects with direct action around human rights violation. He is adept at providing insight and suggestions on organizing projects as he talked about his own work within and outside the realm of policy intervention. He stated clearly that activism doesn't have a particular medium, mode of operation, or location. He alluded to the "grassroots," where organizing means to organize oneself and to prepare others to engage in networking and community activism locally.

As an activist, People's Republic of Mars is internationally and globally minded. His local work in New York has always been connected to immigration, access to healthcare and education, and creating safe community spaces. He invoked international frameworks for thinking critically about our interactions with our rights. In doing so, he challenged the hypocrisy of the United States around implementation of human rights policy and approaches to peacekeeping. Like other study participants, he deferred to international news for diverse information about current social and political events happening around the world.

As an organizer, it is noteworthy that People's Republic of Mars recently created his own organization. In discussing his business plans and objectives, it is clear that he wanted to move beyond the slow grind of policy lobbying and into the realm of direct action, to bring clean water and food to children and schools. He acknowledged the wide array of forms that activism takes that are quieter than the trope of public protest, such as feeding people, teaching, and being of service in local community spaces. As he contemplated the role of Internet organizing and his future work around human rights, People's Republic of Mars demonstrated the expansive vision of empowering individuals and communities with the tools to achieve a healthy standard of living. He used the language of history to challenge power in contemporary struggles for human rights, safety, freedom, and dignity for current and future generations.

Awesome Woman

Awesome Woman articulated her activist identity in many multiple ways. Early in the study, she detailed the concept of an "active activist" and acknowledged that there are a lot of things she refuses to accept about the oppressive and violent ways people talk to and interact with each other. One thing that is noteworthy in conversation with Awesome Woman is the way in which she included competing narratives and counternarratives in a larger conversation about identity politics, rights, and freedoms.

As an activist and a trained performer, she actively pushes into new terrain. While we worked on this study, Awesome Woman's activist actions included international educational travel to South Africa, Feminist Bootcamp, and many other moments of critical cultural programming in and around her university. It is important to note that throughout her participation in this study, she was outwardly critical of the social world that perpetuates prejudice from within university settings. She called for seminars and purposeful learning instead of misogynistic parties with no message that add no value to the school community. She focused a great deal on the struggle around mobilizing women on campus and pointed to the importance of consuming and producing multimedia information as a form of educational activism.

As an organizer, Awesome Woman brought together many perspectives and voices to expand the discourse around equality, identity, and judgment. She worked to grow the Black Student Union, she organized cultural programming around LGBTQ and feminist issues, and she created media to challenge dominant narratives from bigoted status quo discourse spaces. In all of these moments and the numerous others she articulated throughout the course of our time together, she counteracted violent elements in sociopolitical and cultural contexts, created safe spaces, celebrated differences, and offered a powerful message of joyfulness in struggle.

Discussion: Lines of Flight for Peaceable Activist Futures

The youth involved in this study collectively articulate their activist identities in interconnected and divergent ways. Together, the participants each articulated a discursive position that defers judgment so that more open-ended learning and development can take place. As youth activists, they remembered the workshops from youth development organizations as moments of powerful community-based learning. They invited multiple voices as they fought for people they did not know. One question that came up time and again was a query of why ideological lines have to dictate the terms of action for any organizers.

In varying ways, they articulated a collectivist approach to self-mobilization through the creation of safe spaces for anti-oppressive learning. In doing so, youth activists demonstrate that actions are defined as activist in relation to the discussion of their operation. They are activist individuals, responding to social conditions of inequity and injustice. These youth position themselves in ways that are highly political and yet different from one another. This is neither theoretical nor rhetorical. Although there is value in deferral of definitions of organizing and activism, there are implications for articulating, for naming positions, campaigning around values, creating sustainable actions, and investing in community building.

There is much left to debate around the definitions of activism and organizing and the use of the terms. Through Mouffe (1993), it is clear that there are commonalities in the articulation of each of the youth activists. They articulated the need for educative spaces that were safe and inquirybased. They spoke to the influence of family, friends, and community on the organizing work that they do. They shared priorities around immigration, LGBTQ rights, information security, and access to quality education. These major themes are reflective of the current domestic and geopolitical landscape. Beyond policy, they are all defined by the action that they take. Around shared concepts of collectivity and bringing stakeholders together, they are characterized by their orientation as anti-oppressive, radically nonviolent, and morally pluralist. This relates to the ethical notion of alterity out of which Mouffe's writing is based, the recognition that one can only understand one's (shifting) self by understanding the other.

Of course, as a writer and an outsider, I can't say what they intrinsically state by articulating their activist identities every day. They demonstrate through their multiple perspectives and critical approach to research and outreach that there is benefit in not being stuck in a position on an issue. It's not about fixity. It is about identifying in relation to moments of struggle.

The idea of becoming remains crucial here in recognition of the endless equivalences that can be made, because both discourses and subjectivities are always processive. Mouffe's model forces us to focus on the development and construction of individual subjectivities that are able and willing to participate in democratic politics. Specifically, this work involves doing so in ways that contribute to them becoming bordercrossers who politicize issues, recognize and respect difference, and value dialogue toward ethical action.

Significance in and of Articulation in Activist Literacy Research

Articulation theory offers a powerful frame through which to understand participants in relation to their organizing actions, to the elements of their temporal experiences in moments of activist discourse spaces. Following

Mouffe, definitions around activism are not about establishing a baseline against which to determine who qualifies as an activist but rather about how activist identities are constructed in social and historical contexts. In light of this understanding, the idea of positiontaking proves important in alluding to an iterative subjectivity, where individuals choose to act and articulate the self through each moment and event of activism. In practice, the youth involved in this study defined their activist identities as they questioned the prioritization of issues. At the same time, they look at interconnected, multiple topics for informed activism.

As literacy research, the Drop Knowledge Project in New York City adds to understanding about learning in organizing spaces by analyzing the data to identify ways in which youth engage in critical literacy praxis as they build their subjectivity within their communities. By focusing on critical literacy learning outside school, this work adds to research of community-based spheres that possess the capacity to educate young people to think ethically, learn about sociopolitical issues, and articulate their activist identities and their positions through organizing actions. Researching with an ethical and political commitment to democratic and emancipatory forms of educating alongside youth, this research foregrounded the language of social justice organizing as political and historical. As such, a polyvocal focus on dialogic instantiations of critical literacy praxis demonstrated there is much to learn in mapping intersubjective reimaginings, designing peaceable futures, and collaboratively creating articulations of becoming.

REFERENCES

Alinsky, S. (1971). *Rules for radicals*. New York, NY: Random House.
Anderson, G. L., & Irvine, P. (1993). Informing critical literacy with ethnography. In C. Lankshear & P. L. McLaren (Eds.), *Critical literacy: Politics, praxis, and the postmodern* (pp. 81–104). Albany, NY: SUNY Press.
Anyon, J. (2005). *Radical possibilities: Public policy, urban education, and a new social movement*. New York, NY: Routledge.
Apple, M. (1992). The text and cultural politics. *Educational Researcher, 5*, 4–11.
Ardizzone, L. (2007). *Gettin' my word out: Voices of urban youth activists*. Albany, NY: SUNY Press.
Bartoletti, S. C. (1999). *Kids on strike!* Boston, MA: Houghton Mifflin.
Beck, A. S. (2005). A place for critical literacy. *Journal of Adolescent and Adult Literacy, 48*(5), 392–400.
Behring, E. R. (2013). The ethical-political project of social work in Brazil. *Critical and Radical Social Work, 1*(1), 87–94.
Behrman, E. H. (2006). Teaching about language, power, and text: A review of classroom practices that support critical literacy. *Journal of Adolescent and Adult Literacy, 49*(6), 490–498.
Blackburn, M. V., & Clark, C. T. (2007). *Literacy research for political action and social change*. New York, NY: Peter Lang.
Britzman, D. P. (1991). *Practice makes practice*. Albany, NY: SUNY Press.
Borsheim, C., & Petrone, R. (2006). Teaching the research paper for local action. *English Journal, 95*(4), 78–83.

Burbles, N. C., & Berk, R. (1999). Critical thinking and critical pedagogy: Relations, differences, and limits. In T. S. Popkewitz & L. Fendler (Eds.), *Critical theories in education: Changing terrains of knowledge and politics* (pp. 45–65). New York, NY: Routledge.

Christens, B. D., & Dolan, T. (2011). Interweaving youth development, community development and social change through youth organizing. *Youth & Society, 43*, 528–548.

Camino, L., & Zeldin, S. (2002). Making the transition to community youth development: Emerging roles and competencies for youth-serving organizations and youth workers. In T. Burke, S. P. Curnan, J. Erickson, D. M. Hughes, N. Leon, R. Liem, et al. (Eds.), *Community youth development anthology (pp. 70–78)*. Sudbury, MA: Institute for Just Communities, Brandeis University.

Cammarota, J., & Fine, M. (Eds.). (2008). *Revolutionizing education: Youth participatory action research in motion.* New York, NY: Routledge.

Cancian, F. M. (1993). Conflicts between activist research and academic success. *The American Sociologist, 24*(1), 92–106.

Cervetti, G., Pardales, M., & Damico, J. (2001). A tale of differences: Comparing the traditions, and educational goals of critical reading and critical literacy. *Reading Online, 4*(4). Retrieved from http://www.readingonline.org/articles/cervetti/

Chouliaraki, L., & Fairclough, N. (1999). *Rethinking critical discourse analysis.* Edinburgh, Scotland: Edinburgh University Press.

Clary, G. E., & Rhodes, J. E. (Eds.). (2006). *Mobilizing adults for positive youth development: Strategies for closing the gap between beliefs and behaviors.* New York, NY: Springer.

Comber, B. (1993). Classroom explorations in critical literacy. *The Australian Journal of Language and Literacy, 16*(1), 73–83.

Comber, B. (2001). Negotiating critical literacies. *School Talk, 6*(3), 1–2.

Comber, B., & Nixon, H. (1999) Literacy education as a site for social justice: What do our practices do? In C. Edelsky (Ed.), *Making justice our project: Teachers working toward critical whole language practice* (pp. 316–351). Urbana, IL: National Council of Teachers of English.

Comber, B., & Simpson, A. (Eds.). (2001). *Negotiating critical literacies in classrooms.* Mahwah, NJ: Lawrence Erlbaum.

Delgado, M. (2002). *New frontiers for youth development in the twenty-first century.* New York, NY: Columbia University Press.

Delgado, M., & Staples, L. (2008). *Youth-led community organizing: Theory and action.* Oxford, UK: Oxford University Press.

Deleuze, G., & Guattari, F. (1987). *A thousand plateaus.* Minneapolis, MN: University of Minnesota Press.

Durand, T. M., & Lykes, M.B. (2006). Think globally, act locally: A global perspective on mobilizing adults for positive youth development. In E. G. Clary & J. E. Rhodes (Eds.), *Mobilizing adults for positive youth development: Strategies for closing the gap between beliefs and behaviors* (The Search Institute Series on Developmentally Attentive Community and Society) (pp. 233–254). New York, NY: Springer.

Fairclough, N. (1989). *Language and power.* London, UK: Longman.

Fairclough, N., & Wodak, R. (1997). Critical discourse analysis. In T. A. van Dijk (Ed.), *Discourse studies: A multidisciplinary introduction: Vol. 2. Discourse as social interaction* (pp. 271–280). London, UK: Sage.

Flanagan, C. A., & Faison, N. (2001). Youth civic development: Implications of research for social policy and programs. *Social Policy Report: Giving Child and Youth Development Knowledge Away, 15*(1), 1–15.

Flanagan, C. A., Syvertsen, A., & Wray-Lake, L. (2007). Youth political activism: Sources of public hope in the context of globalization. In R. K. Silbereisen & R. M. Lerner (Eds.), *Approaches to positive youth development* (pp. 243–256). New York, NY: Sage.

Fine, M. (1994). *Chartering urban school reform: Reflections on public high schools in the midst of change*. New York, NY: Teachers College Press.

Foucault, M. (1972). *Archaeology of knowledge*. New York, NY: Routledge.

Foucault, M. (1981). The order of discourse. In R. Young (Ed), *Untying the text: A post-structural anthology* (pp. 48–78). Boston, MA: Routledge & Kegan Paul.

Freesmith, D. (2006). The politics of the English curriculum: Ideology in the campaign against critical literacy in The Australian. *English in Australia, 41*(1), 25–30.

Freire, P. (1970). *Pedagogy of the oppressed*. New York, NY: Herder & Herder.

Freire, P., & Macedo, D. (1987). *Literacy: Reading the word and the world*. South Hadley, MA: Bergin & Garvey.

Ginwright, S. (2003). *Youth organizing: Expanding possibilities for youth development*. Occasional Paper Series, no. 3. New York, NY: Funder's Collaborative on Youth Organizing. Retrieved from http://www.fcyo.org/media/docs/4243_Papers_no3_v3.qxd.pdf

Ginwright, S. (2010a). *Black youth rising: Activism and radical healing in urban America*. New York, NY: Teachers College Press.

Ginwright, S. (2010b). *Building a pipeline for justice: Understanding youth organizing and the leadership pipeline*. Occasional Paper Series, no. 10. New York, NY: Funder's Collaborative on Youth Organizing. Retrieved from http://www.fcyo.org/media/docs/6252_FCYO_OPS_10_ScreenVersion.pdf

Ginwright, S., & Cammarota, J. (2007). Youth activism in the urban community: Learning critical civic praxis within community organizations. *International Journal of Qualitative Studies in Education, 20*(6), 693–710.

Ginwright, S., & James, T. (2002). From assets to agents: Social justice, organizing and youth development. *New Directions in Youth Development, 96*, 27–46.

Ginwright, S., Noguera, P., & Cammarota, J. (Eds.). (2006). *Beyond resistance! Youth activism and community change: New democratic possibilities for practice and policy for America's youth*. New York, NY: Routledge.

Giroux, H. A. (2005). *Border crossings: Cultural workers and the politics of education*. New York, NY: Routledge.

Global Kids. (2011). *HRAP grant proposal*. Proposal submitted to New York University Social Venture Competition.

Gonzalez, N. F., Rodriguez, M., & Rodriguez-Muniz, M. (2006). From hip-hop to humanization: Batey Urbano as a space for Latino youth culture and community action. In S. Ginwright, P. Noguera, & J. Cammarota (Eds.), *Beyond resistance! Youth activism and community* change: New democratic possibilities for practice and policy for America's youth (pp. 175–196). New York, NY: Routledge.

Gordon, H. R. (2010). *We fight to win: Inequality and the politics of youth activism.* New Brunswick, NJ: Rutgers University Press.

Gould, P. (1981). Letting the data speak for themselves. *Annals of the Association of American Geographers, 71*(2), 166–176.

Greene, M. (1993). Foreword. In C. Lankshear & P. McLaren (Eds.), *Critical literacy: Politics, praxis and the postmodern* (pp. iii–xi). Albany, NY: SUNY Press.

Greene, S. (Ed.). (2008). *Literacy as a civil right: Reclaiming social justice in literacy teaching and learning.* New York, NY: Peter Lang.

Haj, E., & Abu, T. R. (2009). Imagining postnationalism: Arts, citizenship education, and Arab American youth. *Anthropology and Education Quarterly, 40*(1), 1–19.

Hale, C. R. (2006). Activist research v. cultural critique: Indigenous land rights and the contradictions of politically engaged anthropology. *Cultural Anthropology, 21*(1), 96–120.

Hatch, J. A. (2002). *Doing qualitative research in education settings.* Albany, NY: SUNY Press.

Heinz. (2012). *The power of transformative youth leadership: A field analysis of youth organizing in Pittsburgh.* Retrieved from http://www.heinz.org/UserFiles/File/PghYouthLeadership.pdf

Hirsch, E. D. (1988). *Cultural literacy: What every American needs to know.* New York, NY: Vintage.

Hoose, P. (2001) *It's our world, too! Young people who are making a difference.* New York, NY: Farrar, Straus and Giroux.

HoSang, D. (2003). *Youth and community organizing.* Occasional Paper Series, no. 2. New York, NY: Funder's Collaborative on Youth Organizing. Retrieved from http://www.fcyo.org/media/docs/0228_Papers_no2_v4.qxd.pdf

Hull, G. (1993). Critical literacy and beyond: Lessons learned from students and workers in a vocational program and on the job. *Anthropology and Education Quarterly, 24*(4), 308–317.

Irby, M., Ferber, T., Pittman, K., Tolman, J., & Yohalem, N. (2001). *Youth action: Youth contributing to communities, communities supporting youth.* Takoma Park, MD: The Forum for Youth Investment, International Youth Foundation.

Ishihara, K. (2007). *Urban transformations: Youth organizing in Boston, New York City, Philadelphia, and Washington, DC.* Occasional Paper Series, no. 9. New York, NY: Funder's Collaborative on Youth Organizing. Retrieved from http://www.fcyo.org/media/docs/2789_OccasionalPapers_no9.pdf

James, T., & McGillicudy, K. (2001). Building youth movements for community change. *The Nonprofit Quarterly: Third Sector New England.* Retrieved from nonprofitquartyerly.org

Janks, H. (2000). Domination, access, diversity, and design: A synthesis for critical literacy education. *Educational Review, 52*, 175–186.

Janks, H. (2010). *Literacy and power.* New York, NY: Routledge.

Janks, H. (2013). Critical literacy in teaching and research. *Education Inquiry, 4*(2), 225–242.

Keengwe, J., & Kang, J-J. (2013). A review of empirical research on blended learning in teacher education programs. *Education and Information Technologies, 18*(3), 479–493.

Kincheloe, J. (2006). *Metropedagogy: Power, justice and the urban classroom*. Rotterdam, The Netherlands: Sense Publishers.

Knoblauch, C. H., & Brannon, L. (1993). *Critical teaching and the idea of literacy*. Portsmouth, NH: Boynton/Cook.

Kumashiro, K. (2002). *Troubling education: Queer activism and anti-oppressive pedagogy*. New York, NY: Routledge.

Lankshear, C., & McLaren, P. (Eds.), (1993). *Critical literacy: Radical and postmodernist*. Albany, NY: SUNY Press.

Larson, R., & Hansen, D. (2005). The development of strategic thinking: Learning to impact human systems in a youth activism program. *Human Development, 48*(6), 327–249.

Lather, P. (2001). "The staging of qualitative research": A response to Kathleen Gallagher. *Journal of Curriculum Theorizing, 17*(3), 157–162.

Lather, P. (2007). *Getting lost: Feminist efforts towards a double(d) science*. Albany, NY: SUNY Press.

Lather, P., & Smithies, C. (1997). *Troubling the angels: Women living with HIV/AIDS*. Boulder, CO: Westview/HarperCollins.

Lawrence-Lightfoot, S., & Davis, J. H. (1997). *The art and science of portraiture*. San Francisco, CA: Jossey-Bass.

Leland, C., Harste, J., Ociepka, A., Lewison, M., & Vasquez, V. (1999). Exploring critical literacy: You can hear a pin drop. *Language Arts, 77*(1), 70–78.

Lewis-Charp, H., Yu, H. C., & Soukamneuth, S. (2006). Civic activist approaches for engaging youth in social justice. In S. Ginwright, P. Noguera, & J. Cammarota (Eds.), *Beyond resistance! Youth activism and community change: New democratic possibilities for practice and policy for America's youth* (pp. 21–36). New York, NY: Routledge.

Lewison, M., Flint, A. S., & Van Sluys, K. (2002). Taking on critical literacy: The journey of newcomers and novices. *Language Arts, 79*(5), 382–392.

Lincoln, Y. S., & Guba, E. G. (1985). *Naturalistic inquiry*. Beverly Hills, CA: Sage.

LISTEN, Inc. (2003). *An emerging model for working with youth: Community organizing + youth development = youth organizing*. Occasional Paper Series, no. 1. New York, NY: Funder's Collaborative on Youth Organizing. Retrieved from http://www.fcyo.org/media/docs/8141_Papers_no1_v4.qxd.pdf

Luke, A. (2000). Critical literacy in Australia: A matter of context and standpoint. *Journal of Adolescent & Adult Literacy, 43*(5), 448–461.

Luke, A., & Dooley, K. (2007). Critical literacy and second language. In E. Hinkel (Ed.), *Handbook of research in second language teaching and learning* (Vol. II) (pp. 856–868). New York, NY: Routledge.

Maxwell, J. A. (2005). *Qualitative research design: An interactive approach*. Thousand Oaks, CA: Sage.

Mayo, J. B., Jr. (2013). Critical pedagogy enacted in the gay-straight alliance: New possibilities for a third space in teacher development. *Educational Researcher, 42*(5), 266–275.

McDaniel, C. (2006). *Critical literacy: A way of thinking, a way of life*. New York, NY: Peter Lang.

McLaughlin, M. W. (2000). *Community counts: How youth organizations matter for youth development.* Washington, DC: Public Education Network.

Mira, M. L. (2013). Pushing the boundaries: What youth organizers at Boston's Hyde Square Task Force have to teach us about civic engagement. *Democracy and Education, 21*(1), Article 2. Retrieved from: http://democracyeducationjournal.org/home/vol21/iss1/2

Mokwena, S., et al. (1999). Youth participation, development, and social change: A synthesis of core concepts and issues. *International Youth Foundation.*

Morrell, E. (2004). *Becoming critical researchers: Literacy and empowerment for urban youth.* New York, NY: Peter Lang.

Morrell, E. (2007). Critical literacy and popular culture in urban education: Toward a pedagogy of access and dissent. In C. Clark & M. Blackburn (Eds.), *Working with/in the local: New directions in literacy research for political action (pp. 235–255).* New York, NY: Peter Lang.

Morrell, E. (2008). *Critical literacy and urban youth: Pedagogies of access, dissent, and liberation.* New York, NY: Taylor & Francis.

Mouffe, C. (1993). *The return of the political.* London, UK: Verso.

Nadesan, M., & Elenes, A. (2008). Pedagogical implications of Chantal Mouffe's poststructuralist model of agency and reflexivity. In M. Peters (Ed.), *Naming the multiple: Poststructuralism and education (pp. 245–264).* New York, NY: Bergin and Garvey.

Naples, N. A. (2011). *Feminism and method: Ethnography, discourse analysis, and activist research.* New York, NY: Routledge.

Nieto, S. (1999). *The light in their eyes: Creating multicultural learning communities.* New York, NY: Teachers College Press.

Noguera, P. (2003). *City schools and the American dream: Reclaiming the promise of public education.* New York, NY: Teachers College Press.

O'Donoghue, J. L. (2006). "Taking their own power": Urban youth, community-based youth organizations, and public efficacy. In S. Ginwright, P. Noguera, & J. Cammarota (Eds.), *Beyond resistance! Youth activism and community change: new democratic possibilities for practice and policy for America's youth (pp. 229–246).* New York, NY: Routledge.

Patton, M. Q. (1990). *Qualitative research and evaluation methods.* Newbury Park, CA: Sage.

Petrone, R., & Gibney, R. (2005). The power to speak and listen: Democratic pedagogies for American literature classrooms. *The English Journal. 94*(5), 35–39.

Phelps, S. (2010). Critical literacy: Using nonfiction to learn about Islam. *Journal of Adolescent and Adult Literacy, 54*(3), 190–198.

Pinar, W. (1998). *Queer theory in education.* Minneapolis, MN: University of Minnesota Press.

Pivens, F. F. (2006). *Challenging authority: How ordinary people change America.* New York: Rowman & Littlefield.

Provenzo, E. F., Jr. (2005). *Critical literacy: What every educated American ought to know.* Boulder, CO: Paradigm Publishing.

Reed, D. (1981). *Education for building a people's movement.* Boston, MA: South End Press.

Rogers, R. (2004). *An introduction to critical discourse analysis in education.* Mahwah, NJ: Lawrence Erlbaum.

Rogers, R., et al. (2005). Critical discourse analysis in education: A review of the literature. *Review of Educational Research, 75*(3), 365–416.

Rubin, H. J., & Rubin, I. (2005). *Qualitative interviewing: The art of hearing data* (2nd ed.). Thousand Oaks, CA: Sage.

Santo, R. (2013, February 12). Is making learning? Considerations as education embraces the Maker Movement [Web log post]. Retrieved from http://empathetics.org/2013/02/12/is-making-learning-considerations-as-education-embraces-the-maker-movement/

Seidman, I. E. (2006). *Interviewing as qualitative research: A guide for researchers in education and the social sciences* (3rd ed.). New York, NY: Teachers College Press.

Shah, S. (2011). Building transformative youth leadership: Data on the impacts of youth organizing. New York: Funder's Collaborative on Youth Organizing. Retrieved from http://www.fcyo.org/media/docs/2525_Paper_11_CompleteWeb.pdf

Sherrod, L. (2006). Promoting citizenship and activism in today's youth. In S. Ginwright, P. Noguera, & J. Cammarota (Eds.), *Beyond resistance! Youth activism and community change: new democratic possibilities for practice and policy for America's youth* (pp. 287–300). New York, NY: Routledge.

Singer, J. (2006). *Stirring up justice: Writing & reading to change the world*. Portsmouth, NH: Heinemann.

Street, B. (1984). *Literacy in theory and practice*. Cambridge, UK: Cambridge University Press.

Street, B. (2003). What's "new" in New Literacy Studies? Critical approaches to literacy in theory and practice. *Current Issues in Comparative Education, 5*(2), 77–91.

Strobel, K., Osberg, J., & McLaughlin, M. (2006). Participation in social change: Shifting adolescents' developmental pathways. In S. Ginwright, P. Noguera, & J. Cammarota (Eds.), *Beyond resistance! Youth activism and community change: new democratic possibilities for practice and policy for America's youth* (pp. 197–214). New York, NY: Routledge.

Tobin, J., & Davidson, D. (1990). The ethics of polyvocal ethnography: Empowering vs. textualizing children and teachers. *International Journal of Qualitative Studies in Education, 3*(3), 271–283.

Torre, M. E., & Fine, M. (2006). Participatory action research (PAR) by youth. In L. Sherrod (Ed.), *Youth activism: An international encyclopedia* (pp. 456–462). Westport, CT: Greenwood Publishing Group.

Torres-Fleming, A., Valdes, P., & Pillai, S. (2010). *2010 youth organizing field scan*. New York, NY: Funder's Collaborative on Youth Organizing. Retrieved from http://fcyo.org/media/docs/7697_2010FCYOYouthOrganizingFieldScan_FINAL.pdf

Van Dijk, T. A. (2001). Discourse, ideology and context. *Folia Linguistica, 35*(1–2), 11–40.

Warren, M., Mira, M., & Nikundiwe, T. (2008). Youth organizing: From youth development to school reform. *New Directions for Youth Development, 117*, 27–42.

Watts, R. J., & Guessous, O. (2006). Sociopolitical development: The missing link in research and policy on adolescents. In S. Ginwright, P. Noguera, & J. Cammarota (Eds.), *Beyond resistance! Youth activism and community change: New democratic possibilities for practice and policy for America's youth* (pp. 59–80). New York, NY: Routledge.

Welch, S. (1991). *A feminist ethic of risk*. New York, NY: Fortress Press.

Yee, S. M. (2008). Developing the field of youth organizing and advocacy: What foundations can do. *New Directions for Youth Development, 117*, 109–124.

CRITICAL PRAXIS AND CURRICULUM GUIDES

Shirley R. Steinberg and Priya Parmar
Series Editors

Critical Praxis and Curriculum Guides is a curriculum-based book series reflective of theory-creating praxis. The series targets not only undergraduate and graduate audiences but also tenured and experienced teachers of all disciplines. Research suggests that teachers need well-designed, thematic-centered curricula and lessons. This is accomplished when the school works as a community to meet its own needs. Community in this sense includes working collaboratively with students, parents, and local community organizations to help build the curriculum. Practically, this means that time is devoted to professional development workshops, not exam reviews or test preparation pointers but real learning. Together with administrators, teachers form professional learning communities (PLCs) to discuss, analyze, and revise curricula and share pedagogical strategies that meet the needs of their particular school demographics. This communal approach was found to be more successful than requiring each individual teacher to create lessons on her/his own. Ideally, we would love it if each teacher could create his/her own authentic lessons because only s/he truly knows her/his students—and we encourage it, because it is possible! However, as educators ourselves, we understand the realities our colleagues in public schools face, especially when teaching in high-needs areas.

The Critical Praxis and Curriculum Guides series provides relief for educators needing assistance in preparing their lessons. In the spirit of communal practices, the series welcomes co-authored books by theorists and practitioners as well as solo-authored books by an expert deeply informed by the field. Because we strongly believe that theory guides our practice, each guide will blend theory and curriculum chapters, creating a praxis—all, of course, in a critical pedagogical framework. The guides will serve as resources for teachers to use, expand upon, revise, and re-create.

For additional information about this series or for the submission of manuscripts, please contact either Shirley R. Steinberg at msgramsci@aol.com or Priya Parmar at priyaparmar_24@hotmail.com. To order other books in this series, please contact our Customer Service Department: (800) 770-LANG (within the U.S.); (212) 647-7706 (outside the U.S.); (212) 647-7707 FAX; or browse online by series at www.peterlang.com.